OBJECT LESSONS

100 LESSONS FROM EVERYDAY LIFE

Charles C. Ryrie

Contents

LESSONS FOR EVANGELISM

LESSONS FOR THE CHRISTIAN LIFE

Introduction

Object lessons are a scriptural means of teaching the truth of God (1 Cor. 10:11; Eph. 5:22-32). Scriptural object lessons are based on objects that are easily procured (Matt. 6:28; 18:1-10). Such simple lessons are the most effective (Matt. 5:14-16; Rom. 9:19-21).

Objects should be easy to obtain so that preparation time is spent studying, not shopping. Objects should be simple so as not to detract from the truth; for truth, not trick, is the goal of teaching. Commonplace objects will help the child remember truth better; for if he sees the object at home or in school, he is likely to remember the truth connected with it.

Every effort has been made to keep these object lessons simple, but they are not complete. The teacher is encouraged to take the seed thoughts contained in these pages, nurture them in his or her own heart, and then present them to the class. After reading one, the teacher should pray and think about it, adding an idea or changing an emphasis, until, under the direction of the Holy Spirit, the lesson becomes God's message for that occasion.

In putting out prepared lesson materials, there is danger that the user will think that all the preparation has been done. Not only should these prepared materials be refined for your particular use, but more important than that, there must be individual preparation of heart before they are used.

May the one who said, "Let the children alone, and do not hinder them from coming to Me," be pleased to use these object lessons to win to Himself those children, "for the kingdom of heaven belongs to such as these" (Matt. 19:14).

LESSONS FOR EVANGELISM

1

Wrong Way–Right Way

OBJECT: A road map.

LESSON: "There is a way which seems right to a man, but its end is the way of death" (Prov. 14:12).

PRESENTATION: Not long ago I wanted to go on a trip, so I asked a friend which was the best way to get there. He told me the best road. Then I happened to see another friend and I asked him what he thought. He also told me the best road—but it was entirely different from the way the first friend had said.

Finally I did what I should have done at the first. I went to the Automobile Club and asked them how to get there. They simply got out this map and showed me on the map the right road. Well, I went on my trip and sure enough I arrived at my destination by simply following the road they had marked.

It's a simple matter to take this sort of trip, but how can you find the way to heaven? You might ask a friend, and I'm sure you would get some kind of answer. Then you could ask another friend, and you would undoubtedly get a different answer. What should you do? Who would be right? You ought to do just as I did about finding earthly directions: go where you can get the right answer. That place is the Bible. Do you know what the Bible says about the way to heaven? Listen to the words of the Lord Jesus Christ, "I am the way . . . no one comes to the Father, but through me" (John 14:6). How can you get to heaven? By trusting the Lord Jesus as Savior, for He is the way to the Father; and where the Father is, there is heaven.

2

Air

OBJECT: Yourself and the air around you.

LESSON: To present the Lord Jesus Christ as the gift of God.

PRESENTATION: Have you ever stopped to think, boys and girls, that on every side of you is one of the most wonderful things in all of God's universe? It's about the only thing that is free today, and it's something you can't possibly do without. Do you know what I'm talking about? Surely, the air we breathe. But that is not half so wonderful as another gift God has given us, and that gift is His Son, the Lord Jesus Christ, whom God gave to the world many years ago.

I've just decided something. I simply do not like to take anything from anyone, so I'm not going to take God's air. If I can't buy it, I just won't use it. I'll stop breathing. (*Hold your breath for a while.*) Well, maybe I will change my mind after all and take this gift from God. Didn't I look rather foolish holding my breath? And yet there are probably some of you here today who are still refusing to accept the Lord Jesus Christ as your Savior. When God freely offers eternal life, peace, happiness and heaven, isn't it foolish not to accept them?

But suppose I did want to buy some air to breathe. Do you know where I could go? I don't. And there is no place where you can buy salvation. God's salvation is not for sale; it is a free gift (Eph. 2:8-9). Either you must receive it as a gift and live, or refuse it and die. What would have happened if I hadn't started to breathe again? Why, of course, eventually I would have died. A human being cannot live without air, and you cannot live eternally without Jesus Christ. If you do not take Him as a gift, then God says you must die.

3

An Invitation

OBJECT: A wedding invitation.

LESSON: To present the way of salvation.

PRESENTATION: Look, I have a letter with me this morning, but I think I'll just put it here on top of the piano, and we'll talk about the weather for a while. Of course, I think I recognize the writing on the envelope. (*Walk to the place where you left the letter.*) But I'd rather talk about something else. Maybe I'll look through this hymnbook first. You know, I've had this letter quite a while, but I guess there's no hurry about opening it.

What's the matter? Oh, you want me to open the letter. Well, I guess I might as well. Look at this. It is an invitation to the wedding of a friend of mine. That's kind of him—I think I'll go. Oh, dear, I won't be able to go after all, for the date is past and the wedding is all over. I've missed it. Isn't that a shame?

Boys and girls, do you know what lesson I'm trying to teach you today? It is just this: God has sent us a message that we call the Bible, and in that Bible He has given us an invitation to heaven. But the invitation is only good until Jesus comes, and then it will be too late to accept it. In the meantime this invitation to heaven is absolutely free, for God says, "Let the one who wishes take the water of life without cost" (Rev. 22:17). It is offered to everyone in the world and that surely includes you. Someday, however, it will be too late to accept God's invitation; and just as I missed this wedding, you may miss your chance to go to heaven. Why not open your heart right now to the Lord Jesus and tell Him that you believe that He died on the cross for you and that you trust Him to take you to heaven some day as He promised?

4

Another Letter

OBJECT: An unsealed letter ready for mailing.

LESSON: To illustrate the eternal security of the believer (Eph. 4:30).

PRESENTATION: I brought a different letter along today for the object lesson. Last week, you remember, I had one I had just received; today I have one that I am going to send. You see that it isn't even sealed yet. Perhaps you wonder what's in the letter, and if I should leave it here and go out of the room you would perhaps open it and read it. But if I lick and seal it as I am doing now, you cannot read it, for it is against the law for anyone to open this letter except the one to whom it is addressed. If after I mail this I remember something else I want to put in it, I can't even get it back from the post office. They wouldn't let anyone have it but the person to whom it is addressed.

Did you know that when you accepted Christ, God sealed you? The Bible says that every Christian is sealed by the Holy Spirit (Eph. 4:30). Now the Holy Spirit is God Himself, and I don't know anyone in all the world who could break a seal like that. You could break the law and open this letter, but not even Satan can take away the salvation that God has given you. It's also possible that the glue on this letter will not stick tightly, and the letter will come open before it is delivered; but it is not possible that the Holy Spirit will leave you or ever die. It could also happen that this letter would not be delivered, but if you are a Christian, God guarantees that He will deliver you into His presence some day, for you are sealed until the day of redemption. Isn't that a wonderful salvation?

5

Faith

OBJECT: A chair.

LESSON: To illustrate faith and to present the plan of salvation.

PRESENTATION: Today I want to use this chair as the object lesson. You see, I am quite tired, and I want to sit down in this chair and rest, but I just don't know whether or not I can trust this chair. It looks like a good chair. The wood appears to be solid and all the joints look tight. I think it would hold me, but I'm still a little bit doubtful. Say, have any of you sat in this chair? Oh, you have. Well, did it hold you? It did. But I still wonder if I can believe you.

Boys and girls, do you see what I'm trying to tell you? The Lord Jesus said, "Come to me, all who are weary and heavy-laden, and I will give you rest" (Matt. 11:28), but you will never experience that rest until you come to Him and take Him at His Word. You can look at Him just as I examined this chair, and you will see that He is all that He claims to be. Everything He did on earth proves that He is the only Son of God and the only One who can give rest. You can ask any of us who have trusted Christ for rest from the guilt of sin, and we will tell you that He does satisfy. But you personally will never know this rest until you trust Him. I'll never get any rest from this chair until I am willing to trust it and sit down. (*Do that now.*) If you want rest from sin then you must be willing to trust the Lord Jesus Christ. Just rest on what He did for you when He died on the cross. He meets every claim. Won't you trust Him right now?

6

News

OBJECT: The front page of a newspaper.

LESSON: Salvation is good news.

PRESENTATION: I thought I'd read the paper to you today. No, not the comic strip page, but the front page. I want you to listen to the news of the day. (*Read several headlines, trying to pick out the bad news of the day.*) These are some of the things that the editors of this paper consider the news of the day. You probably noticed one thing outstanding about the news I just read—it isn't very pleasant. It's too bad there isn't more good news in the paper, but there seldom is.

It's a good thing, then, that I brought along some good news for you today. I didn't find it in the newspaper—I found it in the Bible. You have often heard us talk about the gospel. Well, that word simply means "good news" (Luke 2:10). The gospel is good news. What does it say? It says that God in heaven loved men so much that He sent His only Son to this earth to die. Why did He have to die? He had to die to pay the penalty for sin, because God had said that death is the penalty of sin. Since God's Son did not have sin Himself, He could pay for the sins of others. And that is exactly what He did, for when He died He paid for your sin and mine. But, you ask, how can I have all this for myself? The Bible says that it is yours for the asking.

Sometimes our newspapers get things mixed up, and once in a great while they print a correction but not often. However, I can tell you without any doubt that the Bible never gets things mixed up. This good news about the Lord Jesus Christ is just as true as God who can never lie. Won't you believe God's good news today?

7

A Paycheck

OBJECT: A paycheck or some money received in payment for some service.

LESSON: To contrast the wages of sin and the gift of God (Rom. 6:23).

PRESENTATION: I wonder how many of you have ever been paid for doing some job. You know that I work, and so I brought my check along today to use as our object lesson.

Let me tell you about another paycheck. In my Bible I read, "The wages of sin is death" (Rom. 6:23). My employer pays me in money, but sin pays its wages in death. Since everyone is a sinner, everyone receives this paycheck of death.

If I should go to the bank to cash my check and find that the bank has failed and could not pay, do you know what would happen? Very likely the government would step in and cash my check, for the money in most banks is insured and the insurance would cover the loss. That is exactly what happened in regard to your sins and mine. Jesus Christ stepped in and paid the debt of our sins, not because we couldn't die for our own sins, but because He loved us so much. He became our insurance against having to die.

Now instead of death for your sins, you may have complete forgiveness. For in the place of death, the Lord Jesus offers you eternal life. "The wages of sin is death; but the free gift of God is eternal life in Christ Jesus our Lord" (Rom. 6:23). I had to work for this check, but you cannot work for salvation. God says that salvation is for "the one who does not work" (Rom. 4:5). Which will you have—the paycheck of death or the free gift of eternal life? If you want eternal life, then let the Lord Jesus who shed His blood for you come into your heart this very moment.

8

Hell

OBJECT: A sulphur candle (or several matches could be substituted).

LESSON: To warn of hell.

PRESENTATION: Some time ago I walked into my brother's new house and looked around. Of course I was curious and naturally opened the first closet door I came to. Well, I got a whiff of the worst smelling stuff I have ever smelled, for my brother was being sure that there were no moths in his closet. I brought some of this stuff along today. I'm going to light it and let you smell it too, but don't get too close or it will burn your noses and throats.

This is burning sulphur. The reason I brought is along today is not that it kills moths but that it is mentioned in the Bible, and I don't want you ever to forget it. Boys and girls, this burning sulphur is the brimstone that the Bible says is a part of the torment of those who spend eternity in hell. The Bible tells of a lake of fire, which burns with brimstone (Rev. 19:20). It wouldn't be pleasant to spend eternity in a place like that, would it?

Isn't it wonderful that God has provided a way so that none of you will have to go to hell? That way is a person, the Lord Jesus Christ. You see, He came to this earth to die for your sins so that God wouldn't have to send you to hell. Sin is the reason that God is forced to condemn people to the lake of fire burning with brimstone; but if someone would pay for that sin, then God wouldn't have to send anyone there. Someone did pay for your sin, and that person is Jesus Christ. Won't you tell God right now that you want to receive the Lord Jesus into your heart? Believe that Christ paid the penalty for your sins, and you will never be in danger of hell.

9

The Installment Plan

OBJECT: Something to signify a purchase on the installment plan (either a book of payments or simply an advertisement from the newspaper).

LESSON: God settles fully the account of sin when we believe.

PRESENTATION: Today I am going to use for our object lesson something that has become common in our life. What does this newspaper ad say? It offers to let you buy this television set by paying so much down and so much every week. You understand that this means that when you go to get the set you must pay the first amount, and then while you are using it you must pay the rest that you owe in weekly payments. Then, finally, after a long time the set will really belong to you. We call that installment buying.

You know, boys and girls, a lot of people are trying to be saved on the installment plan. They think that they may pay for their sins by offering God a certain amount of good works every week or so. They seem to have the idea that God will erase some of the debt of their sins each time they do something good. I hope none of you has that idea, because if you do you will never be saved.

Do you know how God does settle the debt of sin? Let's see what He says about it Himself. When God saved Abraham He said that Abraham's faith was reckoned to him for righteousness (Rom. 4:3). That means that when Abraham believed, his faith was put on his account as payment for his sins. Now you don't know Greek, in which the New Testament was originally written, but let me tell you that this statement also means that God settled Abraham's account all at once. There was no installment plan on which Abraham was saved! The instant he believed, God fully and forever settled the debt of sin, and God has been doing the same ever since.

10

The Way to Heaven

OBJECT: A strong board, a piece of string, two chairs.

LESSON: To illustrate security in Christ (2 Tim. 1:12).

PRESENTATION: Today we are going to let this chair represent the earth on which we live. Now, the thing we all want is to go to heaven, so we'll let this other chair represent heaven. But, as you can see, there is a gap between the two chairs. That space represents sin, which separates us from our heavenly home. It's a space over which no one in his own strength can pass. Some people try to get across either by overlooking their sins (but the Bible says that all men are sinners) or by their own efforts (but the Bible says that we are not saved by our works).

Wouldn't we be in an awful condition if the Lord Jesus Christ had not come to this world to do something about that gap? You see, when He came He had no sin, and so when He died He could and did pay for your sins and mine. Now there is a way to heaven. We're going to put this board across the chairs to represent Christ, who is the way to heaven (John 14:6).

Now I want to stretch this piece of string between the two chairs and let it illustrate what some people think of Christ. They believe that getting to heaven is like walking a tight rope; they are always wondering if the string will hold them. But God's salvation, boys and girls, is like this strong board—you need never worry whether or not it is going to hold you up. You don't trust in Christ like this (*sit gingerly on the board*); you can trust Him completely, like this (*put all your weight on it*). That is the sort of Savior He is, and that is the kind of salvation He offers you today. Wouldn't you be willing to trust a Savior like that? If so, then just bow your head and ask Him to come into your heart, and then He has promised to take you to heaven some day.

11

Eternity

OBJECT: A cup of sand.

LESSON: To emphasize how long eternity is and to present the way of salvation.

PRESENTATION: Do you know what this is? A cup of sand, of course. How many grains of sand do you suppose are in this cup? You could guess, but I wouldn't be able to tell who would be right, for there are far too many for me to count.

I'm going to take just one grain of sand, and I shall give it to you. Suppose you start out and take this grain of sand to New York. Of course, I want you to walk there, and that would take quite a long time, wouldn't it? When you get there, go to the waterfront and leave this grain of sand; and while you're there, pick up another grain and walk back here with it. When you get here I'll put it in another cup and give you another grain out of this cup so that you can do it all over again. I think you can easily understand that this process could go on a long time before you would have taken all this sand to New York.

Do you know what I am trying to illustrate? I'm trying to show you how long eternity is, for the time it would take you to empty this cup one grain at a time is just this long (*snap your fingers*) in eternity. Don't you think, boys and girls, that it is rather important to know where you'll be all during that time? The Bible says that you will spend eternity either in heaven or in hell, and it also tells you how you can be sure it is heaven. The Lord Jesus Christ said that He would give eternal life to anyone who would believe in Him. Wouldn't you like to receive Him into your heart right now and be sure of spending all eternity in heaven?

12

An Important Day

OBJECT: A calendar.

LESSON: "Now is the acceptable time, behold, now is THE DAY OF SALVATION" (2 Cor. 6:2).

PRESENTATION: This is a very familiar object, isn't it? Do you notice that all the important days on this calendar are marked in red? That is one of the reasons why we have calendars, so that we may know what day it is and what important days are ahead.

But there is one very important day that is not marked on this calendar in the special way that days such as Christmas and Easter are. Do you know what day I'm talking about? I mean today.

Why is today important? It is important because there may never be a tomorrow. It is so easy for us to say that tomorrow we'll do this or that, or next week we are planning this or that. But God says that tomorrow may never come for us (James 4:13-15). That is why today is so important.

But there is another special reason why today is important. That is because today is the day of salvation. Perhaps some of you boys and girls who have come today are not sure that you are going to heaven. Well, you can be sure by simply believing that Jesus Christ, God's Son, died on the cross for your sins. If you will open your heart to Him, He will come in and take away all your sin and take you to heaven some day. But don't put it off until tomorrow or until next week, because today is the day of salvation for you. There is no more important day than today, so won't you make it your day of salvation? Ask the Lord Jesus now to come into your heart and save you.

13

Sinners All

OBJECT: Several children of different sizes.

LESSON: "For there is no distinction; for all have sinned and fall short of the glory of God" (Rom. 3:22b-23).

PRESENTATION: I shall need some of you to help me today. First, I need a very tall person, then the shortest one in the room, and finally several of you who are in between. If you will come to the front I'll use you as the objects.

You all know that the Bible says that all men are sinners, but I suppose many of you think that as God looks down on the human family He sees different kinds of sinners. If we let the ceiling be heaven, then does that mean that this smallest child is a very bad sinner because he is so far from heaven? Does it mean that the tallest fellow is much nearer heaven and therefore not so bad a sinner? Is that the way God looks at the human race? Of course you understand that we're just letting the different heights represent how good or bad a person is.

If you read only part of the Bible verses I'm illustrating today you might think that this was true, but God distinctly says that there is no difference. There aren't good sinners and bad sinners. Everyone is a bad sinner, and everyone in the human race is way down on the level of the lowest and no nearer to God than anyone else. Therefore, everyone needs to be saved just as badly as anyone else. It doesn't make any difference if you've come from the nicest home in town, or if you are a bum; all of you need an equal amount of the grace of God to save you. If you are not saved today, won't you see yourself as God sees you—a low sinner who needs a Savior? Then open your heart to the Lord Jesus and be saved.

14

The World

OBJECT: A bit of dust and a globe or map of the world.

LESSON: To magnify God's love for me.

PRESENTATION: What do you know about the world in which you live? Do you know that it is about twenty-five thousand miles around the earth and that this globe contains nearly two hundred million square miles? I wonder if anyone can guess how much the world weighs. It weighs about six billion billion tons.

But do you know what God says about the size of the world? He says, "Behold, the nations are like a drop from a bucket, and are regarded as a speck of dust on the scales; behold, He lifts up the islands like fine dust" (Isa. 40:15). All of the nations put together are no more than the fine dust on a pair of very delicate scales. I brought some dust, but of course this dust weighs far more than the fine dust the verse is talking about. God's picture of the world is quite different from ours, isn't it?

This is what I want you to think about. If the world is so small in relation to the whole universe—the sun, all the planets, the stars—why do you suppose God sent His Son, the Lord Jesus Christ, to the earth to live and to die? The Bible answers that question clearly. "For God so loved the world, that he gave his only begotten Son" (John 3:16a). It was because He loved me that He sent His Son to die. Why did He love me that much? Simply because He wants me to be with Him in heaven for all eternity. Just think—a little speck like me on this earth that is only dust in God's sight is worth so much that the Son of God came to die in order to take me to heaven!

The rest of John 3:16 tells us how we may be sure of heaven: "Whoever believes in Him should not perish, but have eternal life." Is He your Savior today?

15

What Death Is

OBJECT: A single cut flower or bouquet of cut flowers.

LESSON: To show that death is separation.

PRESENTATION: What do you think of when you think of death? Perhaps you think that it is the end of everything. In a sense physical death is an end. But death doesn't really mean the end; it means separation. Look at this flower. Beautiful, isn't it? Is it alive or is it dead? Well, you hesitate to say it is dead because it looks so much alive. But really, is it alive? No, for it has been cut off the plant. There is no real life in that flower. If you don't believe me that this flower is actually dead, then just wait a few days and you'll see for yourself that it is.

Did you know, boys and girls, that there is a kind of death that is worse than physical death? It's what we call spiritual death, and it is the separation of a person from God. Everyone who is not a Christian is spiritually dead, for he is separated from God. Now, a lot of spiritually dead people look very nice, just like this flower, but they are just as spiritually dead as they can be.

Do you know what it is that causes spiritual death? It's sin. Sin is the thing that cuts us off from God and causes us to die spiritually. Have you ever sinned? Until you are forgiven you are cut off from the life that is in Christ. Would you like to do something about that condition? There is something you can do, and that is to accept Jesus Christ as your very own Savior. He died for your sin, and if you will receive Him into your heart, He will come in and take away all your sins so that you may be alive. "He who has the Son has the life; he who does not have the Son of God does not have the life" (1 John 5:12). How about you today? Are you dead or alive?

16

Rejecting

OBJECT: A photograph of yourself or something you have made or drawn.

LESSON: To show what it means to God for a person to reject Christ.

PRESENTATION: I imagine that you boys and girls did not know that once in a while I like to paint pictures. I'm no artist but I do enjoy trying to do a little painting occasionally, and I thought that perhaps you would like to see something I had painted. There it is. How do you like it?

I'm glad that you all seem to like it. That makes me feel real good. Even if the painting were not so good, you do the right thing when you tell me that you like it. How do you think I would feel toward you if you told me you didn't like it, or if you laughed at it? Then I wouldn't be very happy with you, would I? What do you think I would do if one of you came up here and tried to destroy my painting? Well, I might become quite angry, and you couldn't blame me if I did. What do you suppose my reaction would be if I offered to give one of you my picture and you rejected it? Again I might become angry because you rejected something that I had made myself.

Do you know that God's world, which He made, is like my painting? He made it in order to show you something about Himself (Rom. 1:19-20). When you look around you or up into the heavens at night you ought to see God in it all; and if you don't, then you are saying that He isn't a very good artist, and you are rejecting the picture He has given us of Himself. God also made a plan of salvation so that you could go to heaven. How do you think He feels if you reject Jesus Christ, who is that way to heaven? Look around and see the Creator everywhere. Then look to His Son in faith, and your sins will be taken away. Do not reject Christ. Instead, receive Him today.

17

Ignoring

OBJECT: A dollar bill.

LESSON: To show that ignoring Christ is the same as rejecting Him.

PRESENTATION: Last week we talked about what it means to God to reject His Son as your Savior. Perhaps some of you, who still have not received Jesus into your hearts, think that you are not really rejecting Him by not receiving Him. But I want to show you that ignoring Christ is the same as rejecting Him.

You have often been told that salvation is a free gift. It is something like offering one of you this dollar bill. Here it is. It's free. All you have to do is to take it. There are lots of ways that you can refuse to take it. You can deliberately get up and walk out of the room and by that action show me beyond any doubt that you do not wish this dollar bill. You can come up here and tell me plainly that you don't want my dollar bill. Both of those actions would be outright rejection of my offer, wouldn't they? But there is another way that you can refuse my gift. You can just sit there and ignore me. You don't have to walk out or say one word to me. All you have to do is nothing, and you are refusing my offer. You see, ignoring my gift amounts to the same as rejecting it.

Maybe that's what some of you have been doing about Christ. You are not openly rejecting Him, but you are simply ignoring Him. I said that there are many ways to refuse God's salvation, but there is only one way to get it, and that is to receive the Savior into your own heart. If you would like to do that today, won't you bow your head now and ask the Lord Jesus to come in and save you? Ignoring Him means rejection; receiving Him means salvation.

18

Power

OBJECT: A glass of water.

LESSON: The gospel is the power of God for salvation (Rom. 1:16).

PRESENTATION: How many of you have ever seen the ocean? Do you know that nearly three-fourths of the surface of the world is water? Have you ever wondered who keeps all that water in place? God does (Col. 1:17). Look at this glass of water. It doesn't seem very heavy, does it? How many of you think you could hold this glass of water in your hand with your arm stretched straight out from your side for one minute? Yes, I imagine most of you could do that. How many of you could hold the glass for one hour in that position? How about one day? Even a little glass of water would become extremely heavy to you after even one hour. But think of it, God holds all the oceans in their places all the time. That takes real power, doesn't it?

There's something that takes even more power on God's part. It is the work of salvation. For a holy God to take sinners like you and me to heaven required the death of His Son, but now that the price has been paid God is able to save all who believe in Jesus. That's the gospel, the good news that Christ died for your sins. And that gospel, the Bible says, "is the power of God for salvation to every one who believes" (Rom. 1:16). When you believe on Jesus as your Savior from sin, God promises to take you to heaven, and the carrying out of that promise depends on His power. Don't you think you can trust the One who holds all the oceans and all the worlds in place in this universe? That God loved you enough to send His Son. Won't you receive Him today so that you can know the power of God for salvation?

19

Kerchoo

OBJECT: A common cold.

LESSON: To illustrate the effects of sin and present the way of salvation.

PRESENTATION: Do you know what happened to me this week? Well, the other night I woke up, and my throat was sore, and my head was all stopped up. The next day I felt worse. Finally, you can see what a "beautiful" cold I have this morning. So I thought I'd use my cold today as an object lesson to represent sin.

When you have a cold nobody wants to be around you. People are cordial to you as long as you don't get too close to them; but start talking to someone to his face, and you'll soon be talking to yourself. Boys and girls, that's exactly what sin does— it separates you from God. God loves you even when you're a sinner, but He simply cannot fellowship with you as long as nothing has been done about your sin.

Furthermore, just as this cold of mine may infect you also, so sin is contagious. If you persist in your sin, the older you get the more you will find yourself under its power. Of course, you will influence others to sin. Be careful. If you don't apply the remedy for sin, you'll soon find yourself really sick and miserable.

I'm "doctoring" my cold. The medicine is working, and I expect to be well very shortly. God has given this world and you a remedy for sin. It's His Son, Jesus Christ, who died at Calvary for your sins. Listen to God's prescription: "Believe in the Lord Jesus, and you shall be saved" (Acts 16:31).

Do you want to be saved from your sin today? Then receive the Lord Jesus into your heart. Pills that are left in a bottle don't do any good. You must take them. A Christ who is outside your heart cannot save you. Ask Him to come in and save you from sin.

20

A Stopped Watch

OBJECT: A watch that is stopped.

LESSON: Life doesn't begin until you accept Christ.

PRESENTATION: Look at my watch. It's a beautiful watch, isn't it? Shiny, easy to read, compact—a very nice watch. There's just one thing wrong with it; it's not running. The watch says three minutes to eight, and if I look at it an hour later it will still say three minutes to eight.

Now, this stopped watch is like all unsaved people in the world. They may be very nice people, but there's just one thing wrong. They have not really begun to live because they don't have eternal life. Oh, they're physically alive, but they know nothing about the divine life that God offers to all who will accept His Son as Savior from sin. And, just like this watch, they will stay in that same condition as long as nothing is done about their sins. You don't really begin to live and make progress until Christ comes into your life.

What good is my watch in this condition? Well, it may be a nice ornament on my wrist, but it certainly is not fulfilling the purpose for which it was made. In the same way, an unsaved person may be a very nice person, but he can never fulfill the purpose for which he was created until he becomes a Christian.

No progress—no purpose; that's an awful condition, isn't it? Well, it's very easy to start a watch—wind it. Look, it's running now. That was easy, but only because an expert watchmaker had assembled all the parts in the right way. On your part, it's very easy to become a Christian. All you must do is believe. He sent the Lord Jesus to die on the cross of Calvary. Now all you have to do is believe that He died for your sins. Then God will give you eternal life. Will you do that right now?

21

All-Seeing

OBJECT: None.

LESSON: To emphasize the fact that God sees and knows everything.

PRESENTATION: My, you all look lovely this morning. Everyone is so neatly dressed. The part of you that I can see is very nice. But, you know, I can only see what's on the outside. God sees everything, doesn't He? And that means that He can see not only your clothes, but He also sees your heart. Do you remember what the Bible says? "Man looks at the outward appearance, but the LORD looks at the heart" (1 Sam. 16:7).

God sees everything, everywhere. The Bible says: "For the eyes of the LORD run to and fro throughout the earth that He may strongly support those whose heart is completely His (2 Chron. 16:9). You never do anything, boys and girls, that God doesn't see.

God sees everything; God sees everywhere; and God sees all the time. He sees your actions in the daytime, and He sees them just as well at night. (*If possible turn the lights off so that the room is dark.*) Sit very quietly while the lights are off. I want to read you a verse of Scripture. "There is no creature hidden from His sight, but all things are open and laid bare to the eyes of Him with whom we have to do" (Heb. 4:13). (*Lights on now.*)

Boys and girls, if you've never faced God and opened your heart to His Son, Jesus Christ, who died for your sins, don't try to run away any longer. Believe on the Lord Jesus Christ today and be saved. If you are a Christian, then remember every day that everything you do is seen by your heavenly Father. Live in such a way that you won't be ashamed to have Him see what you are doing.

22

The Wind

OBJECT: The wind or your own breath.

LESSON: To illustrate the work of the Holy Spirit and to emphasize the need of responding to His call.

PRESENTATION: How many of you boys and girls have ever seen
the wind? Why, some of you say you have. Do you really believe you saw the wind? I don't think you did, and I'll show you
what I mean just now. Look, I'm going to blow breath out of
my mouth. There, did any of you see that? Now, let me hold
a piece of paper in front of my mouth. Did you see my breath
that time? No, you just saw the effects of my breath. In the same
way, when the wind blows you don't actually see it, you just see
what it does.

You know, the Lord Jesus said that the Holy Spirit was like
the wind (John 3:8). You cannot see Him, but you certainly
can see what He does in the world. Tell me, just because you
cannot see my breath or the wind, does that mean they are not
real? Of course not. Neither is the Holy Spirit unreal because
you or I cannot see Him. He is a very real Person who does a
very real work in the world.

Have you ever seen a person standing in a cold draft shiver-
ing and yet not doing anything about it? That's rather silly,
isn't it, especially if there is a warm room he could step into or
a warm coat he could put on. Now, boys and girls, the Holy
Spirit is in the world and in this very room today to tell you
that you need to ask Jesus to come into your heart and save you
from all your sins. That's His job today. If you feel the Holy
Spirit telling you that you need Jesus today, don't ignore Him.
Won't you just bow your head and ask the Lord Jesus to come
into your heart and save you from all sin? (Rev. 3:20).

23

Tears

OBJECT: Your eyes.

LESSON: "The blood of Jesus His Son cleanses us from all sin"
(1 John 1:7).

PRESENTATION: How many of you washed before you came to
church today? How many of you like to wash behind the ears?
I guess no boy or girl likes to wash there; but have you ever
stopped to think that there is one place on your body you never
wash? Actually, it's a place on the surface, which is not covered
by clothes, but you never wash it. Do you know what I'm talking about? I'm thinking of your eyes. It doesn't make any difference how dirty you get, you never have to wash your eyes because tears keep your eyes clean day and night.

Washing illustrates a very important biblical truth about salvation: "The blood of Jesus His Son cleanses us from all sin"
(1 John 1:7), and the truth is that the death of the Lord Jesus
continues to cleanse you from sin. Notice the tense of the verb in
that verse—it's present. You are kept saved because the Lord
Jesus keeps on cleansing you from all sin. This doesn't mean
that there is blood in heaven, for the blood in that verse means
the death of Christ, and the death of Christ once for all on Calvary continues in effect day after day.

Isn't that a wonderful kind of salvation to have? It's a salvation that not only erases the sins of the past but takes care of
the sins of today. Just like our tears, the blood of the Lord
Jesus works on our behalf whether we do anything about it or
not.

24

A Uniform

OBJECT: Part or all of a uniform (like a basketball or baseball outfit).

LESSON: To warn professing Christians.

PRESENTATION: What is this clothing that I have today? Yes, it's a baseball jersey. And here's a baseball cap and the pants and socks. As a matter of fact, I have a complete uniform here. Now suppose, boys and girls, that I should put on this uniform, as I'm putting the cap on now. You'd really think I was quite an expert baseball player, wouldn't you? I'm probably the greatest pitcher that ever lived, don't you imagine? What's that? Some of you act like you don't believe me. Do you mean to tell me that a uniform doesn't make a player? Well, you're right. Just because I wear a baseball outfit certainly does not guarantee that I can pitch or even play ball at all.

What makes you a Christian? Is it wearing the uniform? That is, are you a Christian because you look like one and even possibly act like one? Of course not, for a Christian is a person who has taken Jesus Christ into his heart as his Savior, and not one who is putting on something on the outside. Being good does not make you a Christian, just wearing a uniform does not make you a player. God says we are saved by Christ, not by our good works.

Perhaps you would be more convinced that I can play ball if I tell you all about the game. No, you still want to see me in action. In the same way, being able to give all the answers about how to become a Christian does not make you one. You must personally and individually receive the Lord Jesus into your heart so that He can take away all your sins.

How about it? Are you really saved? Or have you just been putting on a front? If Christ is not in your heart, then coming to Sunday school is just like wearing a uniform without being able to play. You may fool others, but you cannot fool God. Are you really saved? If not, or if you are not sure, then right now won't you ask the Lord Jesus to save you from all your sin?

25

A Plane Ticket

OBJECT: A plane ticket, or any transportation ticket, even a bus transfer.

LESSON: Jesus Christ is the only way to the Father (John 14:6).

PRESENTATION: You see that I have here a ticket that will let me ride from Dallas to St. Louis. (*Substitute names to fit the local situation.*) Very soon I'm going to use the ticket, and when I get on the plane and hand it to the stewardess, it will take me all the way to St. Louis, where I'm going to see my father.

I have another ticket here today, too, but it's in my heart; that ticket is the Lord Jesus Christ. I took Him by faith, and He's going to take me all the way to heaven, where I'm going to see my heavenly Father. This plane ticket is all paid for. That's also true of the ticket in my heart. It's all paid for, but at an awful price. Jesus Christ, the Son of God, had to die in order that I, by taking Him as Savior, might get to heaven.

Since I have this ticket to St. Louis, I'd be very foolish not to use it, wouldn't I? Suppose that on the day I planned to leave, you saw me out at the airport, and I started to run along the runway to St. Louis. How far do you think I'd get? I doubt if I would get very far! And yet there are many, many people who are trying to get to heaven by their own efforts. How far do you think they're going to get?

Now, this ticket has a date on it, and I can't use it after that date. Boys and girls, soon the Lord Jesus is coming again, and if you don't have a ticket to heaven in your heart, it will be too late. Is He your Savior today? If not, accept Him now.

26

Believing

OBJECT: A dollar.

LESSON: Faith is necessary to salvation (Eph. 2:8-9).

PRESENTATION: The first boy or girl who comes up here will get this dollar. (*Hold up clenched fist with dollar in it but do not show it. The offer will probably have to be repeated.*) Here comes someone. Let me ask you, do you really believe that I have a dollar here, and do you really believe that I am going to give it to you? Well, you're right. I have a dollar in my hand, and I said that the first one to come would receive it. Since you believed me, you are going to get the dollar.

Do you know what that illustrates? Faith. In this case, faith means simply believing that what I said was true. Do you boys and girls know that Jesus Christ said that not the first one only but anyone and everyone who comes to Him for eternal life will receive it if he will believe in Him? If you have never accepted by faith the Lord Jesus Christ as your own Savior from sin, will you go to Him and do it today?

Our friend had to come for this dollar himself. Just so, you must take Jesus Christ for yourself. No one can do it for you. Now, here's your dollar, just as I promised. You didn't have to work for it, did you? And you can't work for salvation either (Eph. 2:8-9). If you are unsaved, trust Jesus Christ, and He will save you. Let's bow our heads while those who would like to be saved go to Him now in prayer and tell Him that they take Him as their Savior.

27

My Diary

OBJECT: A diary.

LESSON: Your name should be written in the book of life (Rev. 13:8).

PRESENTATION: Today I have my diary with me. Do you know what I keep in my dairy? Well, I write many things in it: important events and interesting things that have happened. I'm going to read a few things to you now. Listen. "July 23—Billy accepted Christ as Savior today. . . . September 6—Two were saved in Sunday school today."

Did you know that God keeps a diary? Do you know what He calls His diary? Well, He calls it the "Book of Life." And do you know what He writes in His diary? He writes the name of everyone who is saved—that is, everyone who has received by faith Jesus Christ as his very own personal Savior.

It doesn't make much difference whether or not your name is in my diary, but it is very important that your name be written in God's diary, the Book of Life. I may lose my diary, but God never loses His. The ink may fade so that you will not be able to read my diary, but that will never happen to God's diary. I may forget to include your name in my diary, but God never forgets.

Oh, if your name isn't in that Book of Life, it can be today if you will only accept God's gift of His Son as your own Savior now. The moment you do that, you will be saved for all eternity, and God will write your name in the Book of Life. If you've never done it, accept Christ now.

28

The Right Combination

OBJECT: A combination lock.

LESSON: The way of salvation is Jesus Christ (Acts 16:31).

PRESENTATION: Here's a combination lock that we're going to try to open today, and we're going to let it represent all unsaved people who are bound by sin. I have a bunch of keys here, and we could try to use them on this lock. Do you think they will work? Of course not.

Well, suppose you try to open it. (*Hand it to someone.*) You can't do it? (*Hand it to someone else.*) Well, you try. We don't seem to be making much progress getting this lock open. Let's see if we can do better in working something out to free the unsaved person from his sin. Will the combination of good works do it? No, for the Bible says, "Not on the basis of deeds we have done in righteousness" (Titus 3:5). Let's try baptism. Will that wash away sins? No, of course not.

I have a piece of paper here with the combination of this lock on it. Do you suppose that if I tried that combination it would open? Well, let's see. (*Open lock.*) There, you see that it works. I also have a Book here that tells me how a sinner can be loosed from his sins. It says, "Believe in the Lord Jesus, and you shall be saved" (Acts 16:31). Does that work? Yes, for God has said that it would, and those of us who have believed know that it does.

Is there any other combination that will work this lock? No, and there's no other way to be saved, for the Bible says, "There is no other name under heaven that has been given among men, by which we must be saved" (Acts 4:12). Could I add to or subtract from this combination and expect it to work? No, and you cannot add anything to what Christ has done for you by dying for your sins. All you have to do to be freed from your sins is to accept right now what He has done for you.

29

Black Paint

OBJECT: A bottle of turpentine; black paint on the tip of one finger.

LESSON: Only the blood of Christ can remove sin (1 John 1:7b).

PRESENTATION: The other day I was painting, and I got some paint on my finger, just as I have today. We're going to let this paint represent sin; everyone born into this world has a sinful heart, for all have sinned, the Bible says (Rom. 3:23). The problem is how to get rid of this sin.

Well, there are some people who try to cover it up like this. (*Close hand tightly.*) You can plainly see what happens—it spreads. (*Paint will be on the palm of the hand when it is opened.*) If I should scratch my face, I would get paint all over my face. We cannot cover up sin from the sight of others and certainly not from the sight of God. What can we do?

The other day when I was painting, the first thing I did after I finished was to try to wash off the paint. I should have known better, because the paint did not come off at all. By your own efforts you won't be able to wash away your sin. People try to do so in many different ways, but they all fail. Some are baptized, some join a church, and some do many good works, but that awful stain of sin still remains.

Let's try this bottle of turpentine. You see what is happening—the paint is coming off, and I don't even have to scrub it. Just so, there is only one way to remove that stain of sin, and that way is by the blood of Jesus Christ, which was shed for you on Calvary's cross. You don't have to do anything. Simply accept Jesus Christ as your personal Savior, and His precious blood will cleanse your heart. Do it right now if you've never done it.

30

A Rubber Band

OBJECT: A rubber band.

LESSON: God's promises and longsuffering are certain (2 Pet. 3:9).

PRESENTATION: Some people say that we Christians are mistaken to expect that the Lord will return. They say that He has been away so long that we can never expect Him to return. But the Bible says that He surely will return (1 Thess. 4:13-18), and it also says that "the Lord is not slow about His promise, as some count slowness; but is patient toward you, not wishing for any to perish, but for all to come to repentance" (2 Pet. 3:9).

Look at this rubber band for a moment. Just as sure as I know that the Lord is going to come, so I know that this rubber band will break if I stretch it enough. Now, I can stretch this rubber band quite a bit before it will break. This verse that I just read said that the Lord is patient, and His patience has been stretched much longer than this rubber band, for the Lord has delayed His coming for almost two thousand years. Rubber bands can be stretched so that they go around larger and larger bundles. That's just the reason the Lord has delayed His coming—so that more people can be saved.

Perhaps there are some here who have put off being saved. Don't put it off any longer, because someday, in the twinkling of an eye, He is going to come. When the last person that is going to be saved is saved, the Lord will come. (*Stretch the band until it breaks.*) Then it will be too late. But it's not too late now if you will accept Jesus Christ as your Savior today. "Behold, now is the ACCEPTABLE TIME; behold, now is THE DAY OF SALVATION" (2 Cor. 6:2).

31

The Lost Pen

OBJECT: A fountain pen or a pencil hidden in the inside coat pocket of a man's coat or in a woman's purse.

LESSON: The unsaved are lost, and Christians must work to win them (2 Pet. 3:9).

PRESENTATION: Somehow I seem to have lost my fountain pen, and I can't find it anywhere. Since this has happened, let's use it for an object lesson and let this lost pen represent every unsaved person, because every unsaved person is lost, too.

I am really very fond of my pen, and I want very much to find it, just as God wants lost sinners to be saved, for He has said that He is "not wishing for any to perish, but for all to come to repentance" (2 Pet. 3:9). Now, it's certain that if this pen is going to be found, I'm going to have to do it. It surely can't find itself. And if you're not a Christian, you can't save yourself. Someone has to do it, and the Lord Jesus Christ is that person.

Let's see if I can find my pen. Yes, here it is, way down in my inside coat pocket. It's very dark down there, but every unbeliever is in darkness many times darker than that in this pocket. Why was I so interested in finding this pen? Because I like it and I want to use it. And God wants to use every Christian to His own glory. He won't force you, but if you will let Him, He will use you. So, if you have never trusted Christ as Savior, do that right now. And if you have already trusted Him as your Savior, give Him your life so that He can use you.

32

Something I Made

OBJECT: Anything you yourself have made. A simple drawing will suffice.

LESSON: Everyone must face his Creator.

PRESENTATION: Do you know where I got the object I am using today? I made it. Since it is mine, I have the right to do anything I want to do with it. If I wish to tear it up, you have no right to protest, because I am the creator.

God created each of you boys and girls, and someday each of you will have to meet your Creator. For some it will be a wonderful occasion; for others, a terrible time of judgment. Which will it be for you?

If you're not sure, let me tell you how you can be saved from judgment. God doesn't want to condemn any of you. He wants to save you, and He wants to do this so much that He sent His Son, the Lord Jesus Christ, to this earth to die for your sins. God must judge sin, but Christ paid for your sins on the cross, and He will take your sin away right now if you will take Him into your heart. If your sins have been taken away, you can meet your Creator unafraid. Will you let the Lord Jesus Christ come into your heart and take away your sin?

33

A Bottle of Medicine

OBJECT: A bottle of medicine.

LESSON: Christ is the cure for sin (Acts 16:31).

PRESENTATION: Not so long ago, I was sick. I don't like to be sick, so I went to the doctor to see if he could do something to help me. After looking me over, he gave me this medicine to take, and he told me that if I would take it I would get well. I have faith in my doctor, and I believed that if I took the medicine I would get well. So I took it and I recovered.

Boys and girls, everyone born into this world has the disease of sin, and everyone would die from this disease if nothing were done for him. But there's a doctor who can cure this disease. He's the Great Physician, and He's the only one who can help sin-sick people. God tells us in His Word that if we believe on the Lord Jesus Christ as our very own Savior from our sin, we will be saved from this horrible thing. "Believe in the Lord Jesus, and you shall be saved, and your household" (Acts 16:31). Now, if you will believe what God says, and take, not medicine as I have here, but a person, Jesus Christ, as your Savior, God will forgive you all your sins. That's simple, isn't it?

Suppose I had bought this medicine, and, knowing that it could cure me, I had refused to take it. You'd think that was foolish, wouldn't you? And yet some of you here today are refusing to take Jesus Christ as your Savior, even though He is the only cure and even though He has paid for your salvation by dying for your sins. Why refuse Him any longer? Why not accept Him today? Bow your head now, and tell the Savior that you believe that He died for you and that you want Him to save you from sin.

34

A Peanut

OBJECT: An unshelled peanut.

LESSON: The way of salvation is through faith.

PRESENTATION: You all know what this is. It's a peanut. But has anyone of you ever seen the nut that's inside? How do you know it's there? Well, there are two ways that you can know. First of all, you can take my word for it that there is a nut inside this shell. You see, I've shaken it, and I can hear that there's a nut inside. Then, second, since all of you have seen other peanuts, you know that they have nuts in them and of course you assume, and quite rightly, that there is a nut in this shell.

Now, boys and girls, this peanut illustrates salvation. You've never seen salvation, so how do you know that there is such a thing? For the same two reasons that you know the peanut is inside the shell. First of all, you have God's Word. He says that if you simply believe that Jesus Christ died for your sins, He will give you salvation. God is never wrong, and He never goes back on His word.

All of you have seen that trusting Christ as Savior works in other people's lives, and consequently it follows that believing on Him will work in your life, too. So if there is anyone here who has never accepted Jesus Christ as his or her very own Savior, do it right now. Other people have tried it and know that it works. But what's more important than that—God has said He will guarantee that salvation will be yours the moment you accept the Lord Jesus as your Savior. Will you trust Him now?

35

Proofs of Life

OBJECT: A young child.

LESSON: There should be evidence of the new life in the Christian.

PRESENTATION: I want one of you to be the object today. Our object looks very much alive, doesn't he? Well, he is alive, but if he were lying down with his eyes closed, it would perhaps be very difficult to tell that he was alive. But I want to show you how you can tell that he has life.

First of all, you saw the object get up and walk to the front. In other words, he acts very much alive. Now, boys and girls, there are many people who say that they are Christians, but they do not act like Christians. The Bible tells us that Christians ought to act differently when they are saved (1 John 2:6); so if they do not, then we may doubt that they are alive spiritually. If the object here didn't move at all, you would wonder if he was alive; and if you aren't living as a Christian should, then perhaps you do not have eternal life.

We also know that the object is alive because he talks. Just so, Christians talk for their Lord and Savior. It makes no difference how young you are, if you are saved you should be talking for the Lord Jesus Christ. When the object opens his mouth he lets people know that he is alive, and if you are a Christian, you should let everyone know that you are a follower of the Lord Jesus. This means that many things have no place in the Christian's conversation.

What about it? Do you have life that comes from God? If you are not walking and talking as a Christian should, then maybe you were never really saved. So if you are not sure, or if you want to be saved, accept the Lord Jesus Christ as your Savior from sin right now where you are.

36

Something Enduring

OBJECT: A faded flower and a bit of dry grass.

LESSON: The Word of God is abiding and true (Isa. 40:7-8).

PRESENTATION: Look at this flower. What has happened to it? It's faded, isn't it? Look at this grass. It's withered and dry, isn't it? Look at my shoes. Look at that bush outside. Look at the chairs. Everything around us is passing away.

But do you know that there is one thing that endures forever and never passes away or wears out? Listen to these verses from the Bible: "The grass withers, the flower fades, when the breath of the LORD blows upon it; surely the people are grass. The grass withers, the flower fades: but the word of our God stands forever" (Isa. 40:7-8). People spend hours and hours raising flowers that fade in a little while, and they spend a great deal of time trying to grow beautiful grass; yet how much time do they—do you—spend reading and studying God's Word, which never passes away?

It is true that flowers look pretty for a while, but after a short time they are no good at all. But that is not true of God's Word. It has been good throughout hundreds of years, and it is still true today. One of the truths of the Word of God is this: if you will accept the Lord Jesus Christ as your own Savior, He will save you from your sins. All God asks of you is to believe that the Lord Jesus died for you. Are you saved today? If not, take God at His word, for His word endures forever.

37

"Be Ye Ready"

OBJECT: A calendar.

LESSON: We do not know when the return of our Lord will occur.

PRESENTATION: I expect that all of you use a calendar rather often. Who can tell me what a calendar is used for? Yes, it tells us where we are with respect to time, and it also points out special, important days. Now, God has a calendar—the Bible—and the next important event on God's calendar is the return of the Lord Jesus Christ.

This calendar that I have here will tell me exactly when Easter occurs, for instance. But God's calendar has not told us when the Lord is going to come again. As a matter of fact, the Bible says just the opposite, for we read, "Of that day and hour no one knows" (Matt. 24:36).

When some special holiday is drawing near, we are reminded in many ways that it is near, and we are urged to make ready for it. At Christmastime, for instance, we buy presents and send out cards. God is reminding us in various ways that the coming of the Lord is very near, and He urges us in His Word to be prepared for it. Matthew tells us, "For this reason you be ready too" (24:44), and John says: "And everyone who has this hope fixed on Him purifies himself, just as He is pure" (1 John 3:3).

When the Lord comes, will you be ready? Of course, if you are not saved, you must accept the Lord Jesus as your Savior before you can be ready. But if you are saved, you must live a pure life, so that when the Lord comes He won't find you doing something you ought not to be doing. So let's remember that any day on this calendar may be the day of the Lord's coming, and let's be ready for Him.

38

A Piece of Bread

OBJECT: A piece of bread.

LESSON: Christ is the Bread of Life (John 6).

PRESENTATION: Look what I have today—just an ordinary piece of bread. In John 6 the Lord Jesus Christ likened Himself to bread. Why could Christ say, "I am the bread of life"? Well, bread is a necessary food, isn't it? Just so, Christ is necessary to everyone. Unsaved people need Christ in order to have eternal life. Saved people need Him every day. Most of you eat bread daily, I suppose, and you need to feed on Christ every day in order that your spiritual life may grow. You need to read your Bible every day, and you need to talk to the Lord in prayer.

Almost everybody eats and likes bread. It is suitable for all. Just so, the Lord Jesus Christ is suited for everybody. He can meet your every need no matter what it is. He can help you if you need salvation and eternal life, for He has said, "He who eats this bread shall live forever" (John 6:58). He can help you if you are saved and need help, for God has said that He will supply all your need (Phil. 4:19). Bread is a satisfying food, and Christ, the Bread of Life, satisfies every need.

Maybe some of you here have never tasted of Christ, the Bread of Life. What's the first step in eating this bread? Yes, taking it into the mouth. And the first step you must take is to take Jesus Christ, not into your mouth, but into your heart. He said, "If anyone hears My voice and opens the door, I will come in to him" (Rev. 3:20).

Will you bow your heads? If you boys and girls who are not saved will open your hearts and take the Bread of Life, you will receive eternal life. Talk to the Lord Jesus about it right now.

39

Heaven

OBJECT: A photograph of some well-known place.

LESSON: What heaven is like.

PRESENTATION: I wonder if anyone recognizes the picture I am holding up right now. Yes, it's a picture of the Grand Canyon. How many of you have ever been to the Grand Canyon? Well, if you have not, then the next best thing is to look at pictures of it, isn't it?

How many of you have ever been to heaven? No one? Well, how many of you have seen a picture of heaven? No one? No, as far as I know, no one has ever taken a photograph of heaven. But someone did see heaven and came back to earth to give us a word picture of it. Do you know who? Well, it was the apostle John. His detailed word picture of heaven is recorded in the last two chapters of the Bible. Let me read to you some of the things he says about heaven. (*Read Rev. 21:1-4, 21; 22:1-5.*)

Doesn't that sound like the most wonderful place you have ever heard of? I wonder how many of you are absolutely sure that you will some day see that place John described? You can be sure, for John tells us who is going to be in heaven (*Read Rev. 21:27.*) All of those and only those whose names are written in the Lamb's Book of Life will be in heaven. Who are those people? Why, they are the Christians, those who have believed on Christ as their Savior. They will populate heaven. You may ask, "How can I belong to that group?" Not by joining this church, for no church has possession of the Book of Life. Not by baptism, for water won't write your name in that book. But by accepting the Lord Jesus Christ into your heart as your Savior from sin, you can be assured that you belong to the group that will be in heaven.

40

No Savior Substitute

OBJECT: A packet of some sugar substitute, such as Sweet 'n Low or Equal.

LESSON: There is no substitute for Jesus Christ as the Savior from sin.

PRESENTATION: Do you recognize this little packet I have in my hand? Yes, it's one of those sugar substitutes that people often put in their coffee, for instance. Perhaps you've seen your folks use one of these products.

People who are dieting use sugar substitutes because they contain less calories than pure sugar. Let me open this packet and pour out a little into my hand. See, it looks like sugar. And it tastes sweet like sugar (taste a little or have someone else taste it). But it isn't sugar.

Do you realize that some people, sometimes even preachers, try to give people a substitute savior. They tell you that you can have your sins forgiven and be sure of heaven by believing this idea or by following that person. The idea that living as good a life as you can will satisfy God is a false savior. Of course, you should live a good life, but that will not take you to heaven. No person, dead or alive, other than Jesus Christ can take away your sins, no matter what anyone says. False saviors may look good and even claim to save, but they are false.

There is one thing sugar substitutes like this cannot do. They cannot be used to bake something. Your mother can't bake a pie with this, because the heat will make the substitute taste bitter, and you wouldn't like the taste of the pie.

All substitute saviors, whether people or ideas, cannot withstand the fires of hell. So don't trust any idea or anyone other than Jesus Christ. He is the true Savior, and if you will receive Him today as your Savior, He promises to forgive your sins and eventually take you to heaven.

41

An Anchor

OBJECT: A picture of an anchor, or a kind of anchor made by tying a piece of rope to something heavy such as a brick.

LESSON: The Lord Jesus has gone to heaven as our anchor (Hebrews 6:19).

PRESENTATION: You know what an anchor does, don't you? If a ship, even a very large one, is tied to an anchor, then it won't drift away. The anchor makes it secure.

Our Lord has gone to heaven where He is an anchor for us. That means we are completely secure. Nothing or no one can break what joins us to Him. I made a kind of anchor to show you today. I'll put this brick behind something so you cannot see it, and I'll hold the other end of the rope that is tied to it. Even though I cannot see the brick, I know it is there whenever I tug on the rope. Just so, we know that our Lord is there for us in heaven, especially when some trouble or difficulty makes us hang onto Him even tighter.

Obviously I can move this anchor I made because the brick is not very heavy. But nothing can move our Lord. Our anchor and consequently our hope in Him is sure and steadfast (Hebrews 6:19).

Our anchor also guarantees that we will go where our Lord is, and He is anchored in heaven. We may drift away for a time, but eventually we will go where He has anchored us. We will have ups and downs in our Christian lives, but because our anchor is already in heaven, we can be sure that someday we will go there to be with Him.

Is the Lord Jesus your Savior today? If so, then He is also your anchor. If not, will you receive Him now?

LESSONS FOR THE CHRISTIAN LIFE

42

The Comics

OBJECT: The comic page from a daily newspaper.

LESSON: To urge the importance of daily Bible reading.

PRESENTATION: I am sure that I do not have to tell you what I have here today. It's the comic page from the paper. How many of you read the comics every day? I see that most of you do. Now let me ask you another question. How many of you read the Bible every day?

Isn't it strange how busy we can imagine ourselves to be when we are reminded of the importance of reading God's Word daily? At least being busy is the excuse most people give. Let's be honest about this. It only takes five or ten minutes to read a chapter from the Bible, and I am sure that all of us can easily afford to spend at least that much time in God's Word.

I know that most of you spend at least ten minutes reading the paper or listening to the radio or watching television every day. Of course there is nothing wrong with doing those things unless they take so much time that there is none left for reading God's Word and praying to Him. If that happens then you had better turn off the radio or television program earlier in order to have time for Bible reading. I know that when some of you miss one of your favorite comics for even one day that you can hardly wait until you see what happens the next day. Don't you think that God's Word deserves the same daily interest?

Suppose we make this a matter of prayer together right now and ask the Lord to help us make time for His Word every single day. I know the Lord will hear and answer such a prayer if you are willing to pray it. Shall we bow our heads and talk to Him about it?

43

My Glasses

OBJECT: A pair of glasses.

LESSON: We need the teaching of the Holy Spirit (John 16:13).

PRESENTATION: Today I am going to use my own glasses as the object. (*A pair may be borrowed, but they should have optical lenses.*) We are going to let these glasses represent the Holy Spirit. Do you know why I have to wear glasses? Simply because I need them in order to see clearly. Do you know what important ministry the Holy Spirit is carrying on today? He is here living inside every Christian to help him understand what the Bible says. Listen to this verse: "But when He, the Spirit of truth, comes, He will guide you into all the truth" (John 16:13). Just as I cannot see without my glasses, so you cannot understand the truths of the Bible without the Holy Spirit.

Wouldn't I be foolish to leave these glasses at home in my dresser drawer when I know that I need them? And yet that is exactly what many Christians do with regard to the teaching ministry of the Holy Spirit—they never avail themselves of His wonderful work.

You know that these glasses were made especially for me, and they aren't much help to anyone else. Any change in my eyes would mean that I would have to get new glasses. So the Holy Spirit works in your heart to meet your special need, whatever it may be. If I may reverently say so, He is for everyone of you a special pair of glasses to help you see and understand the things that are in God's Word. Isn't it wonderful that God has given us this help? If you have trusted the Lord Jesus as your Savior, then the Holy Spirit lives in you, and if you will let Him, He will help you to understand the Bible.

44

Dark Glasses

OBJECT: A pair of dark glasses.

LESSON: Sin colors spiritual perception.

PRESENTATION: Today we are going to have another object lesson about a pair of glasses. But take a look at this pair. You see that this pair of glasses has colored lenses. What did the regular glasses represent? Yes, the Holy Spirit. What do you suppose this dark pair represents? It represents sin that comes into the life of the Christian and colors his outlook so that he cannot see things as they really are. These are Satan's glasses, which he tries to make you wear.

Let me give you an illustration of how Satan works. You know that God does not want His children to lie. But there are Christian boys and girls who sometimes, when they get into trouble, try to squirm out of it by telling a lie. Only they don't call it a lie. They call it a "white lie." Let me tell you that there is no such thing as a "white lie"—all lies are black. What has happened is this: Satan has put a pair of dark glasses on that boy or girl, and he or she doesn't see clearly that the Bible says not to lie (Col. 3:9).

This is a very serious matter, boys and girls, for when sin gets into our lives we are grieving the Holy Spirit, and God tells us not to do that (Eph. 4:30). What about you today? Are you wearing dark glasses that are coloring your ability to understand the Bible? Whatever your dark glasses may be made of—whether temper, or hate, or disobedience, or lying—confess the sin to God right now, and He will forgive you. Then you will be able to see clearly again.

45

Balloon or Brick?

OBJECT: An inflated balloon and a brick.

LESSON: What king of Christian are you in a pinch?

PRESENTATION: I'm going to let the two objects today represent two individual Christians. Don't be surprised if one of them acts much like any Christian you know. This Christian over here (*hold up the balloon*) is the sort of person who talks a lot. We sometimes say he is full of hot air. He can tell you that all you have to do to be saved is to believe on the Lord Jesus Christ; he answers all the questions in Sunday school; he talks big before the other boys and girls about how long he has been a Christian. Do you know anyone like that?

Now this other fellow (*hold up the brick*) is a Christian too, but he is just as solid as a rock. Yes, he also talks about the Lord and answers questions in Sunday school, but what he says he backs up with his life. You can really count on him, for just like this brick, he is solid through and through.

But watch—Satan comes along. He puts some temptation in the path of each of these Christians. Perhaps their schoolmates call them sissies when they begin to tell about the Lord Jesus. Has Satan ever done that to you? What kind of a Christian were you in the pinch? Were you a brick Christian (*pinch the brick*), or a balloon Christian (*pinch the balloon until it bursts*)?

What kind of Christian does the Lord Jesus want you to be in the pinch? Like the brick, of course. But do you know how to be like that? Read your Bible, pray every day to the Lord, and above all, back up everything you say with the way you live. Are you a balloon or a brick Christian?

46

Cleaning Up

OBJECT: Several toilet articles such as those mentioned in the presentation.

LESSON: To emphasize the concern a Christian should have for a clean heart (1 John 1:9).

PRESENTATION: I'm sure all of you know what this is. Yes, it's a washcloth, and of course you use it to wash your face—and also your ears when Mother is watching! How many of you washed your face this morning? Now, what is this? Yes, a toothbrush. How many of you brushed your teeth this morning? Here's a comb. I wonder how many of you used one of these today. (*Other items such as a fingernail file, clothes brush, and shoe brush may be added to the list, but they should all be items used for cleaning purposes.*)

I know that all of you used one or more of these articles this very day, and I suppose that most of you spent quite a little time cleaning up before you came today. But let me ask you a serious question. How much time did you spend cleaning up on the inside today? You know that the Bible says that "man looks at the outward appearance, but the LORD looks at the heart" (1 Sam. 16:7). Don't you think, then, that it's much more important that you be clean on the inside?

But how can you do that? Surely none of these objects will clean the heart. Shall I try the toothbrush or the hairbrush? It would be foolish, wouldn't it? But there is something that will clean the heart, and that is the blood of the Lord Jesus Christ. If you are not a Christian this morning, then simply open your heart to Him, and He will come in and cleanse it from all sin. If you are a Christian and there is sin in your life, all you need to do is to confess it—and that same blood will cleanse your heart so that your fellowship with God may be restored.

47

Secure

OBJECT: Your own hand.

LESSON: "No one is able to snatch them out of the Father's hand" (John 10:29).

PRESENTATION: No, I'm not going to fight with any of you today —my clenched fist is the object lesson. Now I want the smallest one here to try to get my hand open. You can't do it, can you, and if I had something valuable in my hand you wouldn't be able to get it, would you?

Do you know how the Bible describes the position of every Christian? Each one who has trusted Christ is seen to be held tightly in the hand of God (John 10:28-29). You see, I didn't choose the smallest person to try to open my fist just because I was afraid someone else might be able to do it, but I did it in order to emphasize the contrast between the strength of the hand of God and the lack of strength in puny, weak man. I know that there are lots of people who could force me to open my hand, but no one is able to force open the hand of God and attack any Christian who is held securely in it.

Do you know how strong God's hand is? Well, the Bible says that His fingers created all the stars and moon and things we see in the heavens above (Psalm 8:3). Imagine, God did that with His fingers! How strong, then, do you think His hands are? Are they strong enough to hold you secure for all time and eternity? Of course they are.

But there may be someone here today who does not know about such security. Would you like to know how to have it? The Bible says that if you will come to the Lord Jesus Christ and receive Him as your Savior He will freely give you eternal life.

48

Trapped

OBJECT: A mousetrap.

LESSON: To point out the deceitfulness of sin.

PRESENTATION: I've been having trouble with mice at my house this week, so I thought I'd bring along the mousetrap and use it for our object lesson. This is a fine trap. Look at the fine piece of wood from which it is made. I'm sure that it will help catch my mouse. Look at this fine spring that sets the trap off and kills the mouse. I'm sure that plays an important part in catching the mouse. Look how sturdy the whole thing is. No mouse would walk away with a trap like this one. Look what a clever place there is to put the bait. Surely you'll agree that this is a fine mouse trap.

But what catches the mouse? The wood, or the spring, or the sturdiness? No, the cheese. And, you know, it's such a tiny bit of cheese that I wouldn't even know it was there if I tried to make a sandwich out of it. But when that mouse comes up to the trap all he notices is that bit of cheese, and that's all he cares about. Only when it's too late does he realize that the cheese led him to the trap.

Boys and girls, beware that Satan doesn't deceive you into sin by a little bit of his tantalizing cheese. Sin is pleasure (Heb. 11:25), but that moment of pleasure may trap you so that you find yourself in the complete control of sin. Take a good look beyond the bait and realize just how bad sin is and how deceitful it can be. Satan wants to tempt you, but do not underestimate his power, for his traps have attractive bait and they are strong and sturdy. Remember the mousetrap when you go out to play and when you are in school. Don't let anyone tell you that this or that is just a little sin and not very wrong. That's Satan's bait. It is all sin. Don't be trapped.

49

A Grade Book

OBJECT: A teacher's grade book.

LESSON: To demonstrate the principle of the judgment of Christians (1 Cor. 3:11-15).

PRESENTATION: I suppose that most of you boys and girls have seen the object I have today, for I brought along my grade book. I don't have to tell you what this is used for, because you all know too well—especially toward the end of the school year.

But do you know that God has a grade book in which is written the name of every person who has received the Lord Jesus as his Savior? Do you know what He is keeping in His grade book? The Bible tells us that God is keeping a record of all the things that each Christian has done since the day he was saved. (*Read 1 Cor. 3:11-15.*) It's clear from what I've just read that only Christians have their names in this book because they are the only ones who have built on the foundation Jesus Christ. Someday when Jesus comes again He will open up this book and see what kind of things you have done since you were saved. For the good works He will give a reward in the form of a crown, but the bad works will be burned. I wonder what kind of a record you are making in your Christian life.

Please do not be confused about this. This has nothing to do with your being saved. God saves you when you trust His Son as your Savior, but then He requires you to live for Him. This grade book is concerned with your Christian life. Don't forget this grade book, for God who sees everything is surely keeping a grade book of your life.

50

A Love Letter

OBJECT: A letter from a loved one.

LESSON: To encourage the reading of the Scriptures.

PRESENTATION: Do you know what I have here? It's a letter from my father (or mother, wife, etc.). One day this week the postman stopped at my house and left this letter. What do you think I did when he brought it? Do you think I left it lying around on the table unopened? Of course not. I read it as soon as it came. And yet, boys and girls, God has sent you the most wonderful love letter ever written, and many of you have not opened it all week. You know that I'm talking about the Bible, for that is God's love letter to man. Who can give me a verse in the Bible that shows it is a love letter? (John 3:16; 13:34; 1 John 4:10; Rev. 1:5). Just think—God loves *you,* and He loved you so much that He sent His son, the Lord Jesus Christ, to this earth to die for you in order that you might be with Him forever in heaven. That's the love story of the Bible. How could anyone leave a letter like that unopened?

Do you think I threw my love letter away after I had finished reading it? No, I have read it again and again during the week. Don't you think that would be a good thing to do with God's love letter? If you have a difficult time reading, ask Mother or Dad to read the Bible to you. I don't suppose anyone here has read it completely through, but if you have, you can surely read it again and again and find something new each time. Don't you think God's wonderful Book deserves more time, thought, and attention than any love letter you might receive from someone on earth? Will you promise God today that you will begin to read His Book regularly?

51

Mosquito Bites

OBJECT: Some insect repellent.

LESSON: To emphasize the preventive power of the Word of God (Psalm 119:11.

PRESENTATION: I suspect that all of you have been bitten by mosquitoes at some time or other, and you know that isn't very pleasant. Well, I brought something today that keeps mosquitoes away—and it really works. But you know, mosquito bites aren't a bit bad in comparison to something that happens in the life of every Christian. I'm talking about sin in the believer's life, for even after we are saved we still sin. But wouldn't it be great if we could keep sin to a minimum? There is a way, and it is by having the Word of God stored up in our minds and hearts (Psalm 119:11).

Now wouldn't I be foolish if, knowing, for instance, that I was going camping out in the woods, I did not take this repellent along? I'm afraid I would have a lot of bites before morning. Every day you go out into the world where you are constantly exposed to sin. Can you expect your Bible, which is at home on the shelf and may not have been read for days, to protect you from that sin? It just won't work that way. What does the verse say? "In my heart." The repellent has to be on you, and the Word of God has to be in your heart—not in your mother's or Sunday school teacher's—if it is going to do you any good.

There is another important matter to remember. Do you think the repellent I put on last year will do me any good this year? Of course not; it must be applied again and again. In the same way, you must keep reading and keep memorizing the Bible if it is going to keep you from sin. This is God's preventive for sin. Use it, will you?

52

The Shadow

OBJECT: Your own shadow. (If possible arrange your position so that your body casts a shadow in the room.)

LESSON: Every Christian has an influence on others.

PRESENTATION: You'll have to excuse me for standing in this peculiar position, but I want you to be able to see the object clearly. It's my shadow. See it? This represents my influence I have as a Christian.

How many of you have a shadow? All of you, of course. There is not a single person, no matter how young he is, who does not have an influence on others. Do you think I can get away from my shadow? No, everywhere I go in the open my shadow goes with me. Isn't it strange that some Christians think that there are times and places when it does not make any difference how they live, just because they think no one sees them? Don't you realize that everything you do and say affects others? Even here there are some unsaved boys and girls who won't come to Sunday school simply because of the way some of you act around them. What sort of influence is that?

There's another interesting thing about my shadow. Sometimes I'm not even aware that it is there, but it's still there, isn't it? In the same way, even though you may not be aware of influencing others, you can never tell who is watching your Christian life. It is important to live as the Lord Jesus would want you to every moment.

What makes a good strong shadow? Being right out in the bright sun. Do you know what makes a good strong Christian influence? The same thing—only it is spelled differently. It is being right with the S-o-n, and of course I mean your relationship with the Lord Jesus.

53

Weights

OBJECT: A barbell would be ideal; otherwise, any heavy object.

LESSON: Weights of the Christian life (Heb. 12:1).

PRESENTATION: I wonder how many of you have ever run in a race. I wish those of you who have would raise your hands. Now, how many of you are Christians? I see that more of you raised your hands on this question, yet every one of you who says he is a Christian ought to say that he is running in a race. You see, God tells us that the Christian life is a race, for we read in Hebrews 12:1, "Let us run with endurance the race that is set before us."

We aren't having a race today, but the next time I run in one I think I shall carry along with me these weights. What is the matter? Don't you think that will help me win the race? Why not? Is there any law or rule against carrying one of these in each hand while running the race? Of course there isn't. Then why not do it? After all it would give me more exercise. Yes, I know as well as you do that anyone who wants to win isn't going to be weighted down with any unnecessary object.

How about this Christian race? Do you suppose that there might possibly be anything like these weights in it? Yes, there are, and they are not necessarily things that are wrong or against the rules, but they are things that will keep you from being a winner. Maybe it is some word you say, or some place you have a habit of going, or even some close friend. Whatever it is, the Bible says to lay it aside in order that you may be a winner in the Christian life. Being a winner is worth any sacrifice you could make. Ask the Lord to show you any weights in your life and then lay them aside.

54

Unbelief

OBJECT: Choir robe or bathrobe (preferably one that is too small for you).

LESSON: Faith is vital to the life of the Christian (Heb. 12:1).

PRESENTATION: I guess you think that I'm dressed in a rather strange way today, but this is just the way some of you are dressed in your Christian lives. I'll show you what I mean.

God says that the Christian life is like a race, and every boy or girl who is a Christian is in that race. Of course, we are not supposed to lose but rather to win that race, and yet very few do. Do you know what the reason is? Do you remember the lesson about weights or hindrances in the Christian life? That is one reason we lose the race. But there is a second reason, and that is something wrapped around us like this robe. It is unbelief. The Bible says that it wraps itself around us so that we can barely move. How fast do you think I could run dressed like this? Neither can you run the Christian life when you are all wrapped up in unbelief.

What is unbelief? It is simply not letting God have control of everything. In order to be saved you had to let Christ save you, didn't you? You couldn't do it yourself. Neither can you live the Christian life in your own strength; it has to be lived by faith (2 Cor. 5:7), and that means trusting the Lord Jesus for everything. Are Dad and Mother not saved? Then trust God to save them, and ask Him in prayer about it. Ask in faith for a chance to speak to them. Ask for courage to do it, and then believe that God will give you what you have asked for. That's what faith is, and it is absolutely necessary in winning the Christian race. Don't worry about whether or not you have enough faith. Remember in whom your faith is.

55

Shoes

OBJECT: Several different types of shoes.

LESSON: To show the Christian's responsibility to witness.

PRESENTATION: I almost need a box today to bring all the objects for our lesson. Look what I have here. It's a pair of tennis shoes. What does one use these for? For a special purpose, of course, such as for playing tennis or for some other game. But you surely wouldn't wear them to a formal and fancy dinner party, would you?

Here is a pair of track shoes. You see that they have spikes on them, and of course these spikes are necessary in running a fast race. But you wouldn't wear these around the house, would you? Not only would the spikes be bad for the floors, but they would also make walking difficult. (*Other shoes may be substituted or added.*)

Did you know that the Christian has a pair of shoes? His shoes are readiness to tell others about the Lord Jesus, for the Bible says that the Christian's feet are to be "shod . . . WITH THE PREPARATION OF THE GOSPEL OF PEACE" (Eph. 6:15). I hope that none of you are walking around barefooted, for the Lord wants us to be always ready to tell others about Him. That may mean talking directly to your schoolmates or your parents, and it certainly means always living the kind of life that would let everyone know that you belong to the Lord Jesus. It may mean inviting someone to come with you here next week. When you have shoes on no one sees your feet, does he? In the same way, in the Christian walk no one should see you but only the Lord in your life. And yet I hear so many boys and girls saying, "I want my way—I—I," instead of telling others about the Lord Jesus.

56

How To Eat

OBJECT: Some food such as a slice of bread.

LESSON: To emphasize the necessity of reading and meditating on the Bible.

PRESENTATION: Our object lesson today is about something you do at least three times a day. It's eating, of course, and I brought this bread as the object. I wonder if anyone can guess what the lesson is. Well, I want to remind you again of how important it is for Christians to be reading their Bibles. Some of you may be too young to read, but you can apply this lesson by asking Mother or Dad to read the Bible to you. If anyone doesn't have a Bible, I'll give him part of one afterward. But it is important for all of you to read the Word of God.

Watch me eat this bread. (*Eat some of it as fast as possible.*) You know, that's the way some people read their Bibles. How much do you think they get out of it? I think you see my point. If you are going to get as much as possible out of your Bible reading, you must not be in a hurry. Take time when you read God's Word.

Now watch me eat this bread. (*This time eat slowly, chewing well.*) This is not only the proper way to eat, but it is also the proper way to read God's Word. Jeremiah ate the Word of God (Jer. 15:16) and so did the apostle John (Rev. 10:9-10), and that means taking time with your Bible so that you may understand it. Food that is gulped isn't well digested; neither does the Bible when read hurriedly mean much. Take time to think about what you read. In other words, meditate. The Bible itself stresses the importance of doing just that (Psalm 1:2; 119:97).

57

Necessary Parts

OBJECT: A watch or clock.

LESSON: Every Christian has a job to do for the Lord.

PRESENTATION: Once in a while I hear some Christian boy or girl say that he can't do anything for the Lord because he is too small. Sometimes even grown-up Christians won't do anything unless they can have the biggest job or the most prominent place. I want to show you today that every Christian, no matter how small, is important to the Lord's work.

Look at this watch. Don't you imagine that the hands feel pretty important? They are always showing off to everybody! Yes, and God has to have Christians in important places. But now let me take off the back of the watch. Look at that small spring and that tiny wheel. They don't look so important, do they? And yet without those necessary parts the hands on the front wouldn't be useful. Maybe you are a spring in God's work and don't feel important. But you are important in God's program.

You know that the name on a watch means a great deal. Some manufacturers have better reputations than others. You have a name on you too, if you are saved. It is that of the Lord Jesus Christ. But if you are not doing your part, then His name is disgraced. If I buy a certain make of watch and it stops in a month or so, you can be sure that I wouldn't buy the same kind again. Do you think that unsaved boys and girls will want to become Christians if they see that your Christianity doesn't work well?

Remember, will you, that no matter how small a job you may seem to have, it is so important that you do it well. Then others will want to come to believe in the Lord Jesus too.

58

Safe

OBJECT: An egg, a pan, and a hammer.

LESSON: "Your life is hidden with Christ in God" (Col. 3:3).

PRESENTATION: I am sure that some of you think that you are weak Christians, but I want to show you just how safe and secure you are. I brought along an egg to represent a Christian boy or girl. I don't suppose there is anything more delicate and fragile than an egg, so it represents well any of you who think that you are in danger of losing your salvation. Now we're going to put the egg under this frying pan and let that represent what the Bible calls being in Christ. It is simply that safe place in which God puts you when you are saved. Even though you are weak, you are perfectly safe in Christ's care and shelter. Let's just see how safe you are. Suppose the devil taps you just a little bit. (*Strike the pan with the hammer.*) Does that hurt the egg? Suppose he hits you harder. Is the egg still untouched? Suppose he pounds and pounds. Does the egg break?

Let me read the verse for today (*read Col. 3:3*). Do you see what that means? Your life is just as safe as God is. As long as God can take any blow that may come, then you will never lose your salvation. It doesn't make any difference how weak you are, for He is strong. As long as you are trusting the Lord as your Savior, you are absolutely safe from any attack on your salvation.

But perhaps there is someone here who does not have such a secure and eternal salvation. Wouldn't you like to know that you are safe for all eternity? You can know if you will simply believe that Jesus Christ died for your sins on the cross of Calvary. Won't you tell Him just now that you want Him as your Savior?

59

Keeping Clean

OBJECT: A wrapped cake of soap.

LESSON: To emphasize the need of cleansing for the Christian.

PRESENTATION: I'm sure all of you know what this object is used for. The soap ads we see and hear everywhere today make all kinds of wonderful claims about what this soap or that soap will do for us, but, after all, the main purpose of soap is to make us clean. I expect that most of you used some in a bath either last night or this morning before coming to church. That's a good thing to do. No one likes to be around someone who is not clean.

Soap makes us clean on the outside, but what can you do about cleaning up on the inside before coming to church? Well, there is only one way to do that, and that is to confess your uncleanness, or sins, to the Lord and ask Him to cleanse you (1 John 1:9). He has promised that if we confess our sins He will forgive us, and in that verse He is talking to Christians.

How often do you boys and girls take a bath? Once a year? Of course not—you have to bathe more often than that or you would be filthy. How do you think the inside of a Christian looks who only confesses his sins to the Lord once a year? We have to bathe often, and we ought to confess our wrongs just as soon as we know that we have done something that displeased the Lord. Don't let sins accumulate, but confess them right away.

Does this bar of soap do any good all wrapped up like this? No, I have to open it to use it. So, if you are going to have fellowship with the Lord, it doesn't do any good merely to listen to what I have said. You have to use it, and if there is something you ought to confess to the Lord, then why not do it right now? You'll enjoy the rest of the day much more.

60

Ticklish?

OBJECT: Yourself or another person.

LESSON: To emphasize the need for being sensitive to the truth of God.

PRESENTATION: Will someone come and help me this morning with the object lesson? All right, I want you to try to find out where I am ticklish. Go ahead. Tickle me in several places. You see, I'm quite ticklish in some places and not at all in others. Do you know why that is? In some places the skin is very thin and I am sensitive, but in others it is thick and calloused. For instance, on the ball of your foot hardly anyone is ticklish, but just an inch away, under the arch, almost everyone is.

Boys and girls, I hope this little experiment will teach you a very important lesson. The Lord wants us to be very sensitive to all that He says in His Word, and—may I put it this way—He wants us to jump when He speaks. Some Christians aren't this way at all, for their hearts become just like the thick-skinned parts of the body and are not sensitive to sin. The Bible warns Christians against this condition when it says, "DO NOT HARDEN YOUR HEARTS" (Heb. 3:8). That word *harden* means calloused, so God is saying in this verse, "Don't let your heart become covered with calluses." God wants us to be sensitive to sin, just as sensitive as a ticklish person is ticklish. When you do something wrong, God expects you to feel it right away and not to ignore the fact that you have displeased Him. Also God wants you to be sensitive to His leading day by day.

Would you like to know the name of a good heart medicine to keep your heart tender? It's God's Word, the Bible. Reading, knowing, loving, and obeying this Book will keep you sensitive to God's will. "Thy word have I treasured in my heart, that I may not sin against Thee" (Psalm 119:11).

61

A Down Payment

OBJECT: Money with which to buy something from someone in the group.

LESSON: To illustrate the truth of Ephesians 1:14.

PRESENTATION: I notice, John (or Sue), that you have a very nice looking wallet (or purse). Would you please come up and show it to everyone? How would you like to sell it to me? You will? Good. How much do you want for it? All right, I'll buy it; only I don't have enough money with me to pay the full price today. Will you take a dollar from me now and keep the wallet for me until next week when I'll pay you the rest of the money?

Boys and girls, the dollar I just gave John is called a down payment. It serves as a promise, or pledge, that I will pay the remainder, and it also pledges John to sell it to me. It guarantees that the deal will go through and that neither John nor I can back out once the dollar has been given and received.

Similarly, God has given each Christian a guarantee that He will not break His promise to take us to heaven. That guarantee is the presence of the Holy Spirit in our hearts.

I want you to remember two things about this down payment. The first is: Just as I am going to come back next week and get possession of my wallet, so the Lord Jesus is coming back to get us and take us to heaven to be with Himself forever. The fact that the Holy Spirit lives in our hearts is the guarantee that the Lord will do this. The second thing is: While we are waiting for the Lord, we must be careful to live lives that are pleasing to the Holy Spirit, who now lives within us. So let's live in ways that will please Him each day.

62

The Believer's Works

OBJECT: A silver coin and several matches.

LESSON: To show the different kinds of works done by the believer (1 Cor. 3:11-15).

PRESENTATION: We know that no one is saved by works (Eph. 2:9), but only by faith in the Lord Jesus Christ. After Christians are saved, however, works have an important part in their lives. Throughout our Christian lives we are building on Christ, as the foundation, one of two kinds of works—those that will remain or those that will not. When the Lord comes, He is going to judge every Christian according to the works he has done since he was saved. I want to show you what is going to happen at that judgment.

Here comes a believer who hasn't built well. His works are wood, hay, or stubble, and when the fire of God's judgment tries them, here's what happens. (*Light one of the matches.*) All his works burn because they weren't good works, although he himself is saved. Here comes another believer. His works are of gold, silver, and precious stones, and this is what happens when they are judged. (*Light a match under the coin.*) His works abide, and the Lord says that he will receive a reward.

The question for your heart today is: What kind of works am I building? Will they abide or will they be burned? Let's be careful, as Christians, to build works of gold, silver, and precious stones. If you are not a Christian, all the works in the world won't help you. You need a foundation to build on, and that foundation is Jesus Christ. The way to have Him is to receive Him by faith as your Savior.

63

A Bad Light Bulb

OBJECT: A light bulb that has burned out.

LESSON: To show that a little sin may ruin a Christian's testimony.

PRESENTATION: This light bulb looks all right, doesn't it? But there's just one thing wrong with it—it doesn't work. It has burned out. (*If an electric outlet is available, show that the bulb is burned out.*) Today we are going to show how this bulb is like many Christians who have no testimony for the Lord. They are like this bulb—they're not shining for the Lord.

This bulb—although I'm not certain—may have been exposed to the wind and the rain, and yet that didn't cause it to go out. Some of you are too young to have been tested a great deal, but many Christians have to suffer much for the Lord, and yet He brings them through with a brighter testimony for Himself.

Do you know why this bulb burned out? Let me show you. (*If possible, break the glass from around the stem.*) Look at this wire. You see, it's broken, and that's why the bulb won't light. That's just what happens to many Christians. They can withstand many temptations, but some little sin can ruin their testimony for the Lord.

How about you today? Are there little things in your life that are ruining your testimony for the Lord Jesus? When you're out playing, do you fight with other children? Do you do what Mother asks you to do? Are you telling other boys and girls about the Lord Jesus? It may be just a little thing in your sight—it's big in God's sight—but just as it took only a little break in this wire to put the light out, so it may take only one of those sins to put out your testimony for the Lord Jesus Christ.

64

A Good Light Bulb

OBJECT: An ordinary light bulb that is attached, or the bulb in a flashlight.

LESSON: Abiding in Christ is necessary for fruitfulness (John 15:5).

PRESENTATION: Boys and girls, do you think this is a good bulb? You can't tell unless I screw it in, can you? (*Screw it in so that it lights.*) Now do you think it's good? You know it is. This bulb unattached is like many Christian boys and girls. They are saved, but they don't give light for the Lord Jesus. When they look like this (*bulb not lit*) you can't tell if they are Christians or not. But when they are like this (*bulb lit*), you know for certain that they are.

What makes the difference? It's simply this: the bulb doesn't light unless it has contact with the source of power. Our Lord Jesus said, "For apart from Me you can do nothing" (John 15:5*b*). That means that unless you are in fellowship with Him every moment of the day you can't shine for Him. Do you know what breaks our fellowship with Him? Sin. If there is sin in the life of any of you Christian boys and girls today, confess it right now and get back into fellowship with the Lord Jesus so that you may shine for Him.

How does your Christian life look today? Like this (*bulb unscrewed*)? Or like this (*bulb lit*)?

65

A Broken Fingernail

OBJECT: A broken fingernail.

LESSON: To show that fellowship with Christ is necessary to be a testimony for Christ.

PRESENTATION: Look at my fingernail, boys and girls. What's the matter with it? Yes, it's broken. I hit it the other day and was going to cut it off when I realized it would help me teach an object lesson.

When the Lord Jesus was here on earth He said that without Him we Christians could do nothing (John 15:5). Since God has left us here on earth to do things for Him and to be a testimony for our Savior, it is absolutely necessary that we be able to do those things all the time. But we will never be able to have a strong testimony for the Lord unless we are in constant fellowship with Him. This fingernail is no good to me the way it is, and it certainly does not look very nice; it's just like a boy or girl whose fellowship with Christ is broken because he or she is of no use to the Lord.

What do you think I'm going to have to do with this fingernail? Certainly, I'll have to cut it off, and that's exactly what happens to the testimony of a Christian who is not in fellowship with Christ. The Lord Jesus said, "If anyone does not abide in Me, he is thrown away as a branch, and dries up" (John 15:6).

How does your testimony look? Is it like this? (*Show an unbroken fingernail.*) Or is it like this? (*Show the broken fingernail.*) If it's like that, then you had better get back into fellowship by telling the Lord that you've sinned and then keep in fellowship by constantly reading your Bible and by praying. Will you do this right now as we pray silently? Don't be a broken-fingernail Christian.

Hair

OBJECT: Head of hair.

LESSON: To show God's care for His own (Matt. 10:30).

PRESENTATION: How many hairs do you think are on your head? Well, if you have red hair, you have about 90,000. If you have black hair, there are about 103,000. On the other hand, if you have brown hair, there are more than 109,000 hairs on your head, but if you are a blond, you probably have 140,000 hairs.

Each of you has many, many hairs on your head, and I'm sure that if you started to count them you would tire very quickly. But do you know that God knows how many hairs are on your head? Listen to this verse: "But the very hairs of your head are all numbered" (Matt. 10:30).

This verse shows us the loving care of God, who numbered all the hairs of our heads. If God knows how many hairs are on your head, don't you think He also knows every detail in your life? There's no problem in your life that He cannot solve, and there's no need that He cannot meet. If He knows the number of hairs on your head, He certainly knows when you need strength to overcome temptation, or when you need help in telling someone else about the Lord Jesus.

Remember this little lesson, boys and girls. Every time you comb your hair, for instance, remember just how much your heavenly Father cares for you. But also remember that this is true only if you have believed in the Lord Jesus. So if you have never trusted Christ, do that right now.

67

Windows

OBJECT: A window.

LESSON: The Christian needs constant cleansing (1 John 1:9).

PRESENTATION: When that window was first put in, it was very dirty, and someone had to clean it. It couldn't clean itself; someone had to do it. Just so, every person born into this world is dirty with sin, and the only way he or she can be cleansed from sin is to be washed in the blood of Jesus Christ by simply accepting Him as Savior.

How many of you have ever broken a window? You know that you can't patch it so that Mother and Dad won't discover it. You yourself can't patch your sin-wrecked life, either, but Jesus Christ, if He is your Savior, can do more than patch it. He will give you new life. The Bible says that "if any man is in Christ, he is a new creature" (2 Cor. 5:17). If you want new life, accept Jesus Christ as your Savior.

These windows keep getting dirty, and they need to be washed again and again. How many of you have ever washed windows for Mother? Well, Christians need to be clean themselves, too. The Bible says that this should be done "by the washing of water with the word" (Eph. 5:26). This means that you should read the Bible every day and let it point out to you the sin in your life. Then confess that sin to God, and He will cleanse you (1 John 1:9).

When windows get dirty, you can't see out of them, can you? Well, when your lives get dirty with sin—and I'm speaking to Christians now—others can't see Christ in you, so Christians should remember to keep clean by reading the Bible. If you've never been cleansed by the blood of Christ, accept Him now as your Savior.

68

All Dressed Up

OBJECT: You or some child.

LESSON: Be prepared for the Lord's coming.

PRESENTATION: Come up here a minute, will you, Johnny? My, but you're certainly dressed up this morning. Look at that nice suit and those beautiful new shoes. Your hair is all combed, and you're really fixed up. Why is it you're so dressed up this morning? Oh, it's because you knew that you were coming to Sunday school and church. Do you mean to tell me that you don't usually wear these clothes to school and out to play? Of course not.

Well, tell me, why didn't you put your play clothes on this morning? You surely did yesterday, didn't you? Certainly, you knew that today was Sunday, and you prepared for it. You didn't get all dressed up today because you are going to church tomorrow, did you? Of course not. You got dressed up because you were coming to church today.

Suppose, boys and girls, you knew that Jesus was coming back to earth today. Would it make any difference how you acted today? Would you live differently this afternoon if you knew Jesus was coming back tonight? Well, the Bible teaches us that He might come today. How, then, should you be living? If you really expect the Lord to come today, you'll be ready for Him, just like Johnny expected to come to church today and got all dressed up for the occasion. How can you be prepared for the Lord's coming? Well, you must have all sin in your life confessed and forgiven by Him. If you've done something wrong this week, then right now, bow your head, and ask Him to forgive you. Then you will be ready if He comes today.

69

A Dirty Cup

OBJECT: A cup that is clean on the outside but dirty on the inside.

LESSON: We should not be hypocrites.

PRESENTATION: How would you like a nice, cool drink from this cup? Do you really think you would? It is a nice cup, isn't it? And it does look clean. But I've only shown you the outside. Look at the inside. Now, nobody wants a drink.

The Lord Jesus said something about dirty cups and plates. Talking to the Pharisees He said, "You clean the outside of the cup and of the dish, but inside they are full of robbery and self-indulgence. You blind Pharisee, first clean the inside of the cup and of the dish, so that the outside of it may become clean also" (Matt. 23:25-26). The Lord was speaking against hypocrisy—that is, against people who are outwardly one thing and inwardly another. And the Lord spoke very strongly and harshly against that sin, for He hates it.

Suppose we apply this illustration to ourselves. This cup is like the boy or girl who acts very nice sometimes, who may even know all the answers to questions about God, the Bible, and Jesus, but who on the inside has never had his or her heart cleansed from sin. Some are even fooled into thinking that such a person is a Christian, because no one but God can look into a person's heart and see what is there. But God can, and does.

God knows, and so do you. Is your heart clean today? Have you had your sins completely washed away? Is Jesus your Savior from all sin?

A Deposit

OBJECT: Something on which you have placed a deposit, such as an empty bottle of special water, or a tool or machine that you rent from a store.

LESSON: Our Lord wants us to surrender our lives to Him (1 Corinthians 6:19-29).

PRESENTATION: See this bottle. It had special spring water in it, and every so often the delivery man comes and replaces it with a full bottle. Actually the company owns the bottle, and in order to use it I had to give a deposit on it. That is, I gave the company some money that they will give back to me if I quit buying their water and return the last bottle to them. The deposit assures the company that I won't keep the bottle but will return it in order to get my deposit of money back.

Obviously this bottle belongs to the company that sells this spring water. It does not belong to me. Just so, if you are a Christian you no longer belong to yourself, for the Bible says, "You are not your own" (1 Corinthians 6:19).

Do I have the right to keep this bottle? No. Yet many Christians keep their lives for themselves instead of realizing that they belong to the Lord. The deposit I put on this bottle reminds me that the bottle does not belong to me. Likewise, you and I have been bought with a price, and that price was not money; it was the death of the Lord Jesus. In view of the price He had to pay for us, we ought to give back our lives to Him.

If I want a full bottle of water, I will have to let the delivery man take this empty bottle and fill it. If you want happiness and fruit in your Christian life, you will have to let Christ fill your life again and again. Your life belongs to Him. He put a deposit on it. Let Him control it every day.

71

Not Yours

OBJECT: A pencil imprinted with someone's name.

LESSON: "You are not your own, for you have been bought with a price" (1 Cor. 6:19-20).

PRESENTATION: Look at this pencil I have today. Do you see what's special about it? Yes, that's right, it has a person's name printed on it right here where you normally see the brand name stamped. Do you see whose name it is? That's right, this pencil belongs to my daughter, Carolyn. There's her name stamped right on it. How many of you have pencils or pens with your name on them?

Now let me ask you a question that has a very obvious answer. Whose pencil is this? Why, Carolyn's, of course. It's not mine; it's not yours; it's hers. And how do you know? Because her name is on the pencil.

Let me ask you another question. If you are a child of God, to whom do you belong? If Jesus Christ is your Savior, to whom do you belong? The answer is obvious, isn' it? You belong to Christ. How do you know? Because you are a Christian—you have His name.

How do you get a pencil like this? Well, you send some money in to some company, and the company prints your name on the pencil. It costs something to have this done. Just so, it costs something for you to be able to be a Christian and bear the name of Christ in your life. Imprinted pencils don't cost very much, but Christians have been bought with the blood of Christ. It cost the Lord Jesus His life in order that you and I may be called Christians.

What do you think I should do with this pencil? Throw it away? Of course not. I must give it right back to Carolyn because it's hers. I must not keep it. Likewise, if you are a Christian, your life belongs to Christ. Don't throw it away on selfish ambitions. Give it back to Christ, to whom it really belongs.

72

All to Him

OBJECT: The imprinted pencil used in the previous lesson.

LESSON: It is foolish not to give all to Christ.

PRESENTATION: Do you remember the pencil I had last week with Carolyn's name imprinted on it? I hope you remember the lesson—since we have been purchased by the blood of Christ, we belong to Him.

Now, this pencil belongs to Carolyn, and that's quite obvious since there's her name on it as plain as day. Who should have this pencil then? Carolyn, of course. But I have it. As a matter of fact, I've had it in my possession all week. That's not right, is it? And furthermore, I've been using the pencil, too.

I know Carolyn wants her pencil back, because she asked me for it after the lesson last week. But I haven't given it to her. Actually, I rather like her pencil. It writes well. It's still pretty long so there's lots of use left in it. The eraser is still quite good. I think I'll keep it. But Carolyn wants it, and it is hers.

What shall I do? I know. There's a way we can both be satisfied. I'll just break the pencil in two (*pretend to do so*). I'll give her one piece and keep the other. She should be satisfied now, shouldn't she? But, you say, she won't like that. Well, suppose I give her the half that has the eraser on it. That certainly should make her happy (and me too, because I still have part to use). But, you insist, it isn't right. The whole pencil is hers, and actually by breaking it, I would have practically ruined it. I should have given it all to her in the first place.

Do you see the point? The Lord wants all of us, not just some part of our lives or time or energy or money that may be convenient to give Him. If we try to break off part for ourselves, we'll just make a mess of things. Everything we have belongs to Him. We belong to him. Let's give ourselves completely to Him.

73

My Heart

OBJECT: Your own heart.

LESSON: Christ continuously intercedes for us (Heb. 7:25).

PRESENTATION: Last night, boys and girls, as I was lying in bed, I began to think about this heart of mine. It's been beating regularly night and day for many years, and although I seldom stop to think about my heart, I'm extremely thankful that it keeps right on going whether or not I stop to think about it.

While I was thinking about my heart, my thoughts turned to something else that is going on just as regularly as the beating of my heart. Do you know what that is? It is the work that the Lord Jesus Christ is doing—praying for every Christian all the time. The Bible says that "he always lives to make intercession" (Heb. 7:25), which simply means that the Lord Jesus is at the Father's right hand praying for you right now, and He is doing that all the time.

We will never know, boys and girls, how many temptations or trials did not come into our lives because the Lord Jesus was faithfully carrying on this ministry of prayer for us. Isn't it wonderful to have such a Savior? But don't you think that we ought to thank Him for doing this for us? Someday this heart of mine will stop beating, but the Lord Jesus Christ will never stop praying for you. You often hear about people who have "heart failure," but the Lord never fails, and day after day and night after night He prays for you. Right now let's bow our heads and thank our Savior for what He is doing.

74

An Onion

OBJECT: An onion or some perfume.

LESSON: Fellowship with the world shows.

PRESENTATION: I'm not going to show you the object right away. I have it here in my hand behind my back, and I think as soon as I let one of you smell my hand you will be able to tell me what the object is. Will one of you smell my hand? Now you know that the object is an onion.

We're going to learn a lesson from this onion. It represents all the wrong things that Christian boys and girls do. We'll sum them all up and call them "the things of the world." As soon as any of you Christian boys and girls comes in contact with any of the things of the world, then just as the smell of this onion comes off on my hands, so each sin with which you come in contact will come off on your lives.

Do you think that the Lord Jesus likes to have His children smelling like the things of the world? Of course not, but when you do these things, they surely will leave marks on your lives. Moreover, you are saying to the Lord that He cannot satisfy you, but that you prefer to fill up on the things of the world.

So remember, boys and girls, every time you taste of the things of the world, your Christian lives will show it. Onion stain will wash off, and Christ will cleanse your sins if you will confess them (1 John 1:9). If your lives are stained, confess your sins now, and then live a clean life for the Lord Jesus. Don't be an onion-stained Christian.

75

Fish, Salt, and You

OBJECT: A piece of cooked fish.

LESSON: "You are not of the world" (John 15:19).

PRESENTATION: The other night we had some fish to eat for supper, and I saved a piece of it to bring today because as I was eating it a truth I want to share with you came to my own heart. Now this is a sea fish, and it lived in the ocean all of its life. How many years, I do not know, but I do know that during its lifetime that fish got next to a lot of salt in the sea in which it lived. If you have ever tasted ocean water you know how salty it is, and you can easily imagine how much salt that fish must have absorbed.

But, when I took the first mouthful of this fish the other night, the first thing I said was, "Pass the salt." In spite of all the time that fish spent in the ocean it didn't seem to pick up a bit of salt. It wasn't any more salty than if it had lived all of its life in fresh water.

The lesson for those of us who are Christians is this: All of our lives we live in this world. It is just as corrupt and sinful and wicked as Satan can make it. We hear foul talk, we see evil deeds, and we have to associate with corrupt men. Yet the Lord Jesus expects none of that to rub off on us, because we do not belong to this world. We are citizens of heaven. How are your life and testimony? Are they pure or defiled?

76

Growing Up

OBJECT: Two children of different ages and sizes.

LESSON: We should grow in the Lord.

PRESENTATION: I didn't bring my objects with me today because I want two of you to come up here and be the objects. You see that these two children are of different sizes, and I want to show you why some people grow more in the Lord than others do.

First of all, how old are you? You see that these children are different ages. There are some people who have been saved longer than others, and for that reason they have grown more in the Christian life. But there's another reason why both of these children grew. From the time they were born, they have been eating every day. If you don't eat, you don't grow, and the more you eat, the more you grow. Remember that the same thing applies to the Christian life. The more you read the Bible, the more you will grow. If you never read the Bible, you can't expect to grow in the Christian life. Don't be a starved Christian.

But there's something else you must do if you expect to grow either physically or spiritually. If these children did nothing but eat, this alone would not make them grow: they must also exercise. Christians need to exercise, too—that is, they need to work for the Lord Jesus. "But," you say, "I don't know how to work for Jesus." Let me ask you how you learned to play baseball. After someone had explained the game, you had to get out on the field and try it for yourself and keep practicing. It's the same in the Lord's work. Even if you can't pray in public or tell others about the Lord, you have to keep doing it. I'll guarantee that the more you do it, the easier it will become, and the more you do these things, the faster you will grow as a Christian.

How much have you grown as a Christian? Maybe you have not started. Of course, you must be born before you can grow, and you must be born again before you can grow in the Lord. If any of you have never been born again, you can be right now if you will ask the Lord Jesus Christ to come into your hearts. He died for you; He wants to save you. Will you let Him?

77

Hypocrisy

OBJECT: A book with the jacket of a different book on it.

LESSON: Hypocrisy is trying to be something you are not.

PRESENTATION: Say, boys and girls, I want to show you a very good book I have been reading this week. Here it is. You can see by the jacket that it is a book of jungle stories. They're some of the most exciting I have ever read. Let me read part of one to you. Listen: "Take one teaspoon of sugar. . . ." What in the world is this? Why look. I don't have the jungle story book at all. This is a cookbook. Somebody put the jacket of the storybook on top of this cookbook and fooled me into thinking this was the storybook.

A big word will describe what I have just shown to you. The word is hypocrisy. You know the Lord Jesus had some very strong and condemning words to say about hypocrisy and hypocrites—about people who pretend to be one thing on the outside and are quite a different thing on the inside. Nobody likes a hypocrite—just as I did not like it at all when I found that this wasn't the book I thought it was. A hypocrite deceives people and leads them astray, because he says he is one thing and in reality he is entirely different.

Now do you see how this applies to Christians? Sometimes there are hypocrites who pretend to be saved but really are not. But more often hypocrites are found among Christian people who really do belong to the Lord Jesus but who are not living lives that show it. The Word of God says that we should lay aside all hypocricies (1 Pet. 2:1), because such action is very displeasing to our Lord. Will you ask the Lord to help you this week to live a true Christian life?

78

The Finished Product

OBJECT: A book.

LESSON: Each Christian should do his part in the Lord's work.

PRESENTATION: I brought along a book this morning. Because it's something you use every day, it will be easy to remember the lesson. This is the best book that I've ever seen. Isn't it nice looking? Look at that jacket. Of course, I may be a little prejudiced because I wrote it, but I do think it's a very good-looking book. Now I want to use this book to remind you of some things about our Sunday school (or church). This is your church, and you ought to be just as interested in your own church as I am in my own book. It's yours, and there's not one better.

Think a minute of all that went into this book. All I did was to write it. Then the postman took the manuscript to the publisher, and some people in his office checked it to see that I didn't misspell any words and put it into proper form. Then it was sent to the printer and to the binder. Of course someone cut the trees and others helped make the paper it was printed on. Too, someone was drawing the design for the jacket and composing the jacket blurb. Finally, when all the jobs were done, the book was produced—a finished product.

Now the point is that it takes a lot of people to make a Sunday school or church service successful. Someone has to prepare the lessons or sermons. That's like writing the book. Some sing in the choir; some usher; some lead in prayer. Someone has to tell others about the service just as someone has to sell my book. It doesn't do any good to have thousands of copies of this book stacked in some warehouse, does it? Perhaps your job is to bring someone to church. All of us have to pray, for without prayer we cannot function. Tomorrow morning when you pick up your books at school, will you remember to pray for Sunday school next Sunday?

Tearing Down or Building Up?

OBJECT: A rose in bloom.

LESSON: A Christian should not tear things or people down
(Phil. 4:8).

PRESENTATION: I need someone to help me with the object lesson today. All right, you come up and help me. Do you see this
rose? Now, I'm going to take my watch off and time you while
you do something. I want you to pick all the petals off the rose
one at a time, and we'll see how long it takes you. All right,
ready, go.

That took exactly twenty-one seconds. Very good. Now I
want to time you while you do something else. This time I want
you to put all the petals back on. Ready? Go. What's the matter? You can't do it?

Now, boys and girls, this is the lesson I want you to remember
today. It's always much easier to tear down than to build up.
I'm speaking to you who belong to the Lord because a lot of
Christians have never learned this lesson. They go around
thinking the meanest things they can and saying the most un-
kind words to others, and in every way they tear down the
character of other people. A Christian shouldn't act that way.
His mind, mouth, and manner should always be filled with
things that build up. Listen to this verse from Philippians 4:
"Finally, brethren, whatever is true, whatever is honorable, whatever is right, whatever is pure, whatever is lovely, whatever is of
good repute, if there be any virtue, and if there is anything worthy
of praise, dwell on these things" (v. 8). Does that sound like
tearing down or like building up?

Remember this lesson this week, and when you're tempted to
say or even think something that is not nice or right, ask the
Lord to help you put that thought out of your mind.

80

Strength in Unity

OBJECT: A piece of paper and a large book like a telephone book.

LESSON: Why we should join a church.

PRESENTATION: A lot of you boys and girls are Christians, aren't you? You already have accepted Jesus as your Savior from sin, and you know for sure that He has come into your heart. That's the most wonderful thing in the world, and it makes you sure that some day the Lord Jesus will take you to be with Him in heaven. But, in the meantime, you have a life to live on earth, and you want to live it for His glory.

One thing that will help you in this life is to associate yourself after you are saved with other Christians by joining a church. Now we don't join a church because we think the Lord works only through churches, but because we find strength and help for our lives from other Christians. After all, a church is not a building; it is a group of people who have trusted Christ as their Savior and who are organized to carry on His work. A group of people joined together in this way can carry on the work better than if each tried to do it himself.

Look at this piece of paper. Is there anybody in the room today who couldn't tear it in half? Of course not. That's very easy to do. Now look at this telephone book. Is there anyone here who can tear this in half? I doubt it. Look how difficult it is to tear. Do you know the reason? It's simple, isn't it? When you put together a number of sheets of paper, each of which is easy to tear, you cannot tear them when they are bound together. And that's an illustration of what I've been talking about today. Alone, you can do a lot for the Lord, and it certainly is important that you do all you can do individually for Him every day, but often together we can do more. Also when we're together it's more difficult for Satan to attack us and tear us apart. You should belong to a church, and you should attend, support, and work for that church. God says we must not forsake the assembling of ourselves together (Heb. 10:25).

81

Light Bulbs

OBJECT: Several light bulbs of different sizes.

LESSON: The witness of every Christian is important.

PRESENTATION: I wonder if you ever felt that it wasn't very important whether or not you witnessed for the Lord. "After all," you may have said, "I'm just one person," or "I'm too young and small," or "What can I do to lead others to Jesus?" Now look at this light bulb. It's a big 150-watt one. There's no question about how important this bulb is or what a big light it furnishes.

Now look at this one. It's just a 60-watt one. Well, you say, now you're getting down to my size. All right, have you ever stopped to count how many bulbs of this size you have in use at home? You probably have just one or two big ones, but perhaps a dozen or more smaller ones. They are rather necessary, aren't they? Now look at this tiny one. It's a night light. Not very big, but very important if the whole house is dark except for this one light. Suppose this little light said, "I'm not very important. Folks can get along without me. I don't think I'll shine at all."

Do you see the point? Maybe you are not a big preacher. That's all right. God may make you one some day. But even if you're only a night light, your faithful witness, even though you think it isn't very strong or big, might mean the difference between the salvation or the fall of some soul. Wouldn't you like to ask the Lord right now to help you be a good testimony for Him everywhere you go this week?

82

Walking

OBJECT: You.

LESSON: The Christian life is a walk of faith.

PRESENTATION: Did you know, boys and girls, that every day you do something that God uses as an illustration of the Christian life? That something is walking, for our whole Christian life is called a walk. As a matter of fact it is called a walk of faith (2 Cor. 5:7), which is just the same as saying a walk, or life, that is in total dependence on God and His power.

Have you ever analyzed your process of walking? Well, let's do that today. Look at me now. When I want to walk I simply place one foot in front of the other, but every time I do that I am putting all my faith on the foot that is not in the air to hold me up. You see, when I lift my right foot I am trusting my left one to hold me until the right one reaches the floor again. Every time I take a step, I do it in faith that the one foot will hold me. Walking is an act of faith.

The Christian life is also of faith, and the Lord Jesus wants you to live your life depending on Him. If you're tempted to lose your temper, why not try depending on Him to help you control it? If you need help in telling others about Jesus, why not depend on Him for it? That's what faith is—dependence on someone or something else. And the Christian life is a life of dependence.

Try it this week, will you? Walk by faith in your risen Lord.

83

The Temperature

OBJECT: A thermometer.

LESSON: How to take your spiritual temperature.

PRESENTATION: How would you like to have your temperature taken today? Not your physical temperature, but your spiritual temperature. I want to see if any of you are sick. All right, open your mouths, and I'll put the thermometer in by asking you a few questions.

First of all, did you read your Bible every day this past week? Of course, if your daddy or mother read it to you in a family group you may answer yes to the question. If you didn't read it every day, then answer with the number of days you did read it.

Second, did you pray to the Lord regularly every day this past week? Again, if you have family devotions you may answer yes to the question. Actually, however, all of you are about old enough now to pray by yourselves too, even if you do have family devotions.

Third, what about your life this week? Did you try to live the way a Christian boy or girl should? When you had a chance to speak a word for the Lord, did you do it? This will be a very hard question to score, but I think you know well enough what a Christian ought to be like to be able to answer correctly. Be honest now.

What's your grade on this little quiz? Is it anywhere near 100? It ought to be. You know, even the temperature of your body to be normal should be nearly 100. Maybe someone is saying, "What difference does it make? I won't die spiritually if my temperature isn't normal." That's true, for if you are really saved, you are saved eternally. But listen while I read to you what God thinks about Christians whose temperature is below normal. (*Read Rev. 3:16.*) Just as you don't like a lukewarm drink of water, God can't stand a lukewarm Christian. Maybe we ought to check our temperature a little more often. Suppose you watch yours this week as you try to live for the Lord.

84

A Compass

OBJECT: A compass.

LESSON: The Word of God is our guide.

PRESENTATION: How many of you know what this is? How many have ever used a compass before? If you have, you know that it can be very useful, especially if you are lost.

You know, the Word of God is like a compass because it's a guide for our lives. When you hold the compass level, it points to the north; therefore, you can tell in which direction you are headed. That's exactly what the Bible does, too, boys and girls. It points to God, to Christ, to heaven, to right living now. As you read it you can tell which direction you are heading. If the Lord Jesus is not your Savior, then God's compass says that you are heading in the direction of hell. If you are a Christian and you are lying, cheating, gossiping, or disobeying your parents, God's Word says that you are not headed in the direction of right Christian living.

Once in a while a compass will not point north. That happens when a lot of metal is near, which tends to pull the needle away from the magnetic pole. There's nothing wrong with the compass itself—it's just that something has come between it and the North Pole. Sometimes people can misinterpret the Word of God, too. It's not that the Word is wrong or has changed its meaning. But sin has come between God and the person who is reading it, and that sin may cause you to think you are going in the right direction when you really are not. In such a case you must correct the thing that is causing the deviation by confessing your sin to the Lord.

Remember, God's Word is always true, but in order to understand it aright, you must not have unconfessed sin in your life when you read it. Then if you read it and live by it, you will be guided unerringly into right paths—into God's paths.

85

Ask the Author

OBJECT: A note that you have written to someone in the audience.

LESSON: The Holy Spirit has been sent to teach us the meaning of the Bible (John 16:13-15).

PRESENTATION: *Let the person to whom you wrote the note come to the front with it and carry on with you a conversation similar to the following.*

PUPIL: There's something in this note you wrote me that I don't quite understand.

TEACHER: All right, I will tell you what it means. What is it that you don't understand?

PUPIL: It's this sentence right here.

TEACHER: Well, it means this. . . . Do you understand now?

PUPIL: Yes, thank you very much.

TEACHER: Tell me, why did you come to me and ask about this note? Why didn't you ask one of your friends?

PUPIL: Actually I did ask someone else if they understood what you meant, but since he didn't know, I thought I'd better ask you. After all, you're the one who wrote it, and of all people you should know what you mean.

TEACHER: You're quite right. There's no better person you could have asked than me, since I was the author of this note.

Boys and girls, who wrote the Bible? Yes, a lot of men, but all of them under the direction of the Holy Spirit (2 Pet. 1:21), so actually the Holy Spirit is the author. Jesus said before He left the earth that He would send the Holy Spirit to help every Christian to understand the Bible (John 16:13-15). Since the Holy Spirit lives in every Christian, you can go to Him at any time. So as you read your Bible, ask Him to help you understand what you're reading.

86

A Mirror

OBJECT: A small mirror.

LESSON: It is important to read the Old Testament (1 Cor. 10:11).

PRESENTATION: You all know what this object is, don't you? Yes, it's a small mirror. Why do you use a mirror? Well, sometimes you use it to look at yourself in order to see if your hair is combed or your face is clean. But there's another use for a mirror that I want you to think about today. Sometimes you use a mirror in order to see what is behind you. The best example of this use is the mirror in your automobile.

For the same reason, boys and girls, the Bible records many of the stories in the Old Testament. God wants us to know how He dealt with His people in former days so that we may know how He will deal with us today. The New Testament says that these things happened in former days as examples to us who are living today (1 Cor. 10:11). For instance, you can tell from Old Testament stories what will happen when a Christian marries an unsaved person, for just as Israel always had trouble when she mixed with foreigners, so you will have difficulty if you marry an unsaved person. You also can tell from the Old Testament what God thinks of worshiping idols (Exod. 32).

What would you do if you were driving along in a car and saw a reckless driver bumping cars? Why you'd get out of the way. Just so, if you read in the Old Testament how Satan attacked men, you will be warned so it won't happen to you. But, if you're going to be warned, you have to read the Old Testament and learn from the experiences the people had in those days. So whenever you hear or read these accounts in the Old Testament, ask the Lord to help you to learn the lesson He was trying to teach them, so that you will not make the same mistakes they did.

87

Time Is Running Out

OBJECT: A timer such as you might have around the kitchen.

LESSON: Christ is coming soon (Matt. 24:33).

PRESENTATION: Have you ever seen Mother use a timer like this when she's boiling eggs or baking a cake? Or perhaps you've used it to time a long-distance phone call. And if so, you remember that when the bell is almost ready to ring or the sand has almost gone all the way through the glass, you quickly finished up everything you had to say and got ready to hang up. Or sometimes Mother would open the oven and look at the cake and say, "It's almost done!" Then the timer would go off.

You know, this world is running according to God's timetable, and we are very near one of the most important events in all time. I'm talking about the return of the Lord Jesus to take believers to heaven to be with Him forever (1 Thess. 4:13-18). When this great event happens, believers who have died will be raised from their graves, and believers who are living will be changed in an instant and given new bodies.

What difference should it make that Christ's coming may be very near? Well, we don't quit what we're doing and sit out in some field waiting for Him! We make sure that each day we live a life that is pleasing to Him. Then whether He comes today or tomorrow or the next day, we'll be ready and anxious to see Him.

88

Water, Water Everywhere

OBJECT: A glass of water.

LESSON: The Noahic Flood was very forceful.

PRESENTATION: I want one of you big, strong, he-man boys to volunteer to help me today with the object lesson. All I want you to do is to hold this glass of water for a little while. Only I want you to hold your arm stiff and straight out to your side while you're holding the glass. Easy, isn't it? At least right now it is. But just keep holding it.

That's just a little glass of water he's holding. Can you imagine how much water there was on the earth during the Flood in Noah's day? It rained for forty days, but the water was on the earth an entire year, and during the Flood water came from above and from below (Gen. 7:10-11). You remember, too, that the water covered Mount Ararat, which today is 17,260 feet above sea level. That's a lot of water. How's your arm feeling holding just a glass of water?

Water weighs something, doesn't it? I imagine many of you have carried a bucket of water to wash the car or something. A bucket full of water is a lot heavier than an empty bucket, isn't it? Can you imagine how much weight was dumped on the earth when the Flood came? We know that everything that wasn't in the ark died, but what do you suppose happened to the bodies of people and animals that died? With all the upheaval of the earth and rocks and mountains and with all the weight of the water, they must have been pressed in the rocks. The traces and remains of those animals are the fossils that are found everywhere, and they are the result of this tremendous pressure that the water of the Flood created on the earth.

How does your arm feel now? Ready to put the glass down? Even today about 70 percent of the surface of the earth is water, and it is Jesus Christ who "upholds all things by the word of his power" (Heb. 1:3).

89

Mind Your Mind

OBJECT: A real or toy hard hat such as construction workers use.

LESSON: We need to guard our minds.

PRESENTATION: Have you ever walked by a large construction job? If you have, you probably noticed that the men working all wore a hard hat like the one that I have here today. Too, there were signs posted around the site which said, "Do not enter unless wearing hard hat." Workers have to wear these hats to protect their heads from injury. They don't wear steel vests or iron pants, but they do wear hard hats.

God, too, recognizes the importance of protecting the head. When Paul describes the armor that the Christian wears, he speaks of the helmet of salvation (Eph. 6:17). You see, we aren't saved just from the neck down. Salvation affects our minds also, for after we are saved we have new thoughts, new ideas, new outlooks. But the devil is powerful, and that's why we need to keep protecting our minds all the time with the helmet of salvation.

What would happen if a brick fell on a man who was wearing a hard hat? Nothing, and he would just go on working. Likewise, if your mind is always set on doing the will of God, then Satan's attacks won't hurt you a bit. You'll just go on living for the Lord. Paul put it this way: "Be transformed by the renewing of your mind, that you may prove what the will of God is, that which is good and acceptable and perfect" (Rom. 12:2).

The mind controls the body, so it's important to keep your mind on the right things. Don't let impure thoughts in, because they may result in impure actions. Don't think evil things. Think on what is good (Phil. 4:8). Try minding your mind this week.

90

On Growing Up

OBJECT: Any kind of seed.

LESSON: "Whatever a man sows, this he will also reap" (Gal. 6:7).

PRESENTATION: It's springtime again, and in the spring people begin to think about planting grass or flowers or gardens. So I thought we might learn a lesson today from these few seeds that I brought along. You know, the Bible talks about sowing seed—that is like your life—when it warns that whatever you sow you will reap. If I sow this corn, which is what I have in my hand, then I don't expect to get tomatoes, do I? The same principle works in your life. If you sow little lies, you will reap big lies and lots of trouble with them. If you continue to refuse to accept Christ as your Savior, you may grow up and never receive Him. If as a Christian boy or girl you sow irreverence in God's house by little whispers, you may reap a disregard for even attending services in God's house. When you sow evil you reap evil, and when you sow good things you will reap a good character.

"But," you may be saying, "any wrong thing I do now is awfully little and really can't amount to much." Look at this seed. Just a little thing, isn't it? But when it is planted, it will grow into a very large stalk of corn. Yes, the little sins you are doing now will grow into big sins in later years, and the good things you do, even though they seem very small and unimportant, are very important because they will reap for you a life well-pleasing to God. You see, it is extremely important that you pay careful attention to all the details of your everyday life. What you are now is what you will become when you grow up.

What kind of seeds are you sowing?

91

Joined Together

OBJECT: Several pieces of a jigsaw puzzle, including two pieces that fit together.

LESSON: Be preparing now for a good marriage.

PRESENTATION: Look at all these pieces of this jigsaw puzzle! How will I ever put them together? How many of you have ever worked a jigsaw puzzle? It's hard, isn't it? But remember how delighted you were when you found pieces that fit? "Here's the one!" "This one fits!" And you joined the pieces together into one beautiful picture.

You know, when the Lord Jesus talked about marriage, He said that a man and a woman should be joined together to fit perfectly just like those pieces of the puzzle. That's what the word *cleave* means in Matthew 19:5). When a man marries, he is joined to the woman he marries so that the two become one, so close is the union.

Now I know that some of you couldn't care less about marriage right now. But you will be before very long! May I suggest some things you should be doing now so that when you find the right one you will have a good, solid, happy marriage?

First, once in a while ask the Lord to guide you in this matter of marriage, even though it may seem a long way off now. From among all the people in the world, you want God to lead you to the right partner. Second, remember that you can never fit one piece from one jigsaw puzzle with any piece from a different puzzle. It just won't work. Likewise, you cannot even think about marrying someone who is not a Christian, because it won't work. And finally, keep yourself pure and your ideals high, and wait for God's time and choice. Then your marriage will fit together as it ought.

92

My Aching Foot

OBJECT: A small pebble.

LESSON: The Bible teaches truths about dating and marriage.

PRESENTATION: It's a wonderful thing to have friends, isn't it? God is interested in friendship so much that some day He wants you to find someone who will mean so much to you that you will want to marry that one and live together the rest of your lives. Naturally, then, God is interested also in the friends you have now and the boys and girls some of our older young people are dating right now. He's so interested in fact that He has taken the trouble to tell you some things about these relations with each other in His Word.

For one thing, God does not approve of marriage between a Christian and one who is not a Christian (2 Cor. 6:14). Make no mistake about it, such a marriage will not work. You should have unsaved friends in order that you may win them to Christ, but not with any thought of marrying one. "Well," you say, "that really doesn't make too much difference, does it? After all, we get along so well in everything else, and on Sundays we'll each go our own way." The fact that you are of differing religious faiths may not seem much to you now, but believe me, it will become a very big problem later on. Let me illustrate.

Look at this tiny pebble. You wouldn't think it could cause any trouble. Let me put it in my shoes like this. Why, I hardly feel it. Look, I can walk clear across the room, and it doesn't even bother me. But, how do you suppose my foot will feel to-night if I leave this in all day? You're quite right, I'll certainly have a sore foot. A little thing can be very annoying after a long time.

Now do you get the point? Little differences in friendship may not seem important now, but when you walk through life with that little thing, it can become very annoying. Just be sure that God is leading you in all your dates, and you won't need to worry, because He makes no mistakes.

93

When Your Dog Wags Its Tail at You

OBJECT: Your pet dog.

LESSON: Don't let friends flatter you into doing something wrong.

PRESENTATION: How many of you have a pet dog at home? A lot of you do. I've had several during my lifetime, and they have been wonderful pets to have around.

Probably you have some rules for your dog. For instance, he cannot eat his food anywhere but in the kitchen. No jumping or lying on the furniture. And no getting fed from the table. (I confess when I was a kid that I used to feed my dog food I didn't like from my plate when my folks weren't looking!)

But dogs know very well how to get around those rules. They sit by your chair while you're eating and wag their tails, hoping you will give them a bite of what you are eating. Or when you're sitting comfortably in a big chair watching TV, your dog will sit on the floor right in front of you, looking up sadly and wagging his tail, hoping you'll break the rules and invite him up into your chair. And often you do.

Sometimes we have friends like that. They know that as Christians we have certain rules we should follow. We do certain things, and we do not do certain things. But they sometimes beg us to do things we know a Christian should not do—or ask us not to do things we know a Christian should do. They make something we know is wrong seem very inviting, and sometimes we give in.

Be careful. Don't let friends talk you into doing what you know the Lord does not want you to do. Let's live by the rules that God gives us in the Bible.

94

A Light Switch

OBJECT: A light switch attached to the wall, or use an unattached replacement switch if you have it.

LESSON: Christ is always present in a believer's life.

PRESENTATION: Let me walk over to the light switch on the wall, because it is going to serve as our object lesson today.

The switch is in the "off" position right now, so of course the light it controls is off too. Now I'll turn it on. How do you know it's on? Because you see the light.

In each one of you who is a Christian, the Lord Jesus lives. He is "on" in your life. How can people know that? Because they ought to be able to see Him in what you do, how you talk, how you behave. When they do, then they know that He is there.

I can turn this light off by throwing the switch. But you cannot turn the Lord Jesus out of your life. He is there to stay. Now I could put a black, plastic trash bag over the light, and then you might think it is off. But really it is still on; it is just covered up so that no light shines through. Even though the Lord will never leave you, you can "cover Him up" so that nobody knows you are a follower of His. You can cover Him up, but you cannot turn Him off.

If I cover up this light it will do no more good than if it were off. That's true of your Christian witness as well. So rather than do that, "let your light shine before men in such a way that they may see your good works, and glorify your Father who is in heaven" (Matthew 5:16).

95

A Hole in Your Sock

OBJECT: A sock with a hole in it.

LESSON: To remind of some things that make holes in our Christian lives.

PRESENTATION: Look at this sock (show only a part of it that has no hole). It looks great, doesn't it? But let me show you the rest of it. Wow, see that big hole in the heel! And here's another one in the toe. If you wore this sock, you would soon rub a blister because your heel has no protection.

You sock is like your Christian faith. If it is whole, w-h-o-l-e, then you will enjoy good protection from all the corruption around you in this world. If your faith has a hole, h-o-l-e, then the world can get to you and hurt you.

Paul prayed for the believers at Thessalonica that he might "complete" or "mend" (for that's what the word means) what was lacking in their faith (1 Thessalonians 3:19). He wanted their faith to have no holes in it.

How can we have and keep a strong Christian life? Read the Bible or have your parents read it to you. Memorize some verses from the Bible. When you are tempted, pray that the Lord will help keep you strong. Learn more about God in Sunday school and church. Don't be afraid to let others know you belong to Christ. Keep strengthening your faith so that it looks like this (hold up the whole part), not like this (hold up the hole).

96

Underneath Are His Everlasting Arms

OBJECT: Yourself (or someone strong enough to cradle a child in his arms).

LESSON: To illustrate God's protection (Deuteronomy 33:27).

PRESENTATION: I need one of you boys to help me today. A small one, preferably. You'll see why in a minute. Come here to me, please.

You and I are going to illustrate a verse in the Old Testament. It says, "Underneath are the everlasting arms." This is one of God's promises to Israel to be their protector in times of trouble, as He is for us as well. God said that His arms would be underneath His people. So will you let me pick you up and hold you in my arms? Here we go!

In this position you won't stumble. You don't even have to walk by yourself. I am carrying you. If anyone should try to jab you, all I have to do is hold you a little tighter, or turn my back, and you will be protected. This is a nice, safe position, isn't it?

Now stand up. Suppose I were to try to put my arms on top of you. You would have to lie down so that I could easily place my arms there. (Do this if it is convenient). But watch out! I can also easily push down on top of you and hurt you. So it's a good thing that God did not say "on top are the everlasting arms."

I could place my arms in front of you or behind you while you are standing up. Those positions would offer some protection, but you wouldn't be safe from stumbling. Neither would you feel so secure or loved as when you were held in my arms.

So the next time you have trouble that is not your fault, remember that your heavenly Father holds you in His arms to assure you of His love and protection.

97

Flipping Coins

OBJECT: You will need four or eight or sixteen coins.

LESSON: To show the accuracy of the prophecies of the Bible.

PRESENTATION: Here's a coin. If I flip it once I will get either heads or tails. If I flip it twice, then I will get either (1) two heads, (2) two tails, (3) heads then tails, or (4) tails then heads. Right? So the chance of getting two heads in a row is one in four. Or let's do it this way. Four of you come here. I'll give each of you a coin, and all of you flip it twice. Chance says one of you should get two heads or two tails.

Suppose I want to try to get three heads or three tails in a row. Chance says that will happen one time in eight. Four more of you come up here, and all eight of you flip three times, and we'll see what happens.

Suppose I want to try for 30 heads in a row. The chance of that happening is one in more than a billion. Now there were fewer than a billion people living on the earth at the time Christ was born. So if all of them had coins and flipped them 30 times, not one would have come up with 30 heads in a row by chance.

There are more than 30 predictions in the Bible about the life and death of Christ. Could they have all come true by chance? The answer is no. But they all did come true, and that shows that God inspired the Bible so that it is true. Since we see that the predictions that have come to pass happened just as they were prophesied, we can trust all the rest of the Bible as well—the promises, the predictions not yet fulfilled, the history, everything. The writers did not guess about what they wrote, nor did they just hope it was true. God was guiding them so that everything they wrote was accurate. You can trust your Bible.

98

Who Controls You?

OBJECT: Yourself.

LESSON: To show that a Christian controlled by God will live differently.

PRESENTATION: For a moment I'm going to act and talk like someone you might see on TV. (Stagger, lurch, and talk like a drunk person). Who am I imitating? That's right, a person who is drunk.

Why does a person who has had too much to drink act so differently? Simply because he or she is under the control of the alcohol in his body. The alcohol affects his ability to walk in a straight line. That's why the police will ask a person they suspect of drunkenness at the scene of an accident to try to walk in a straight line. If he can't, then likely he is drunk and will be arrested.

A drunk person cannot talk right either. He will slur his words and sometimes say words you can't understand. Again, it is the alcohol in his system that affects his speech that way. A drunk person cannot think straight. That's why he will often do unreasonable things.

When you became a Christian, God came to live in your life. His presence in your body should make you act differently and talk differently and think differently. Just as alcohol controls a drunk man and makes him different, so God should control your life and make you different. Alcohol in a person's system controls that person in bad ways. Christ in your life can control you in good ways. If you will let Him control you, then people will see that you belong to Him because of the change in your life.

The Bible says that we are not to get drunk with wine; rather we are to be controlled, or filled, with God (Ephesians 5:18).

99

Wrong Label

OBJECT: A can of food from which you have removed the label and replaced it with a label from a different can of food.

LESSON: John 13:34-35.

PRESENTATION: I brought a can of food today to show you something important about the Christian life. What do you think is inside this can? What does the label say? It says that I have a can of blueberries. Good. I like blueberries, so I think I will open the can and taste a few. (Open the can). But look! These aren't blueberries. It's a can of spinach. I don't like spinach, so I'm really disappointed. Actually, I think I'll just throw the entire can away.

I wonder what happened. The label said blueberries, but when I opened it I found spinach. I'll confess to you what happened. I changed the labels before I came today. I took a label off a can of spinach and put it on the can of blueberries.

The Lord said that people will know we are His disciples because we love one another. It's as if you were a can full of Christianity, and the label should say, "This is a Christian because he loves people." But sometimes we switch labels. We put on labels of anger, rebellion, bad language, and so on. We are still Christians. The contents of the can haven't changed, but no one will know what's really on the inside of our lives because they can see only the outside. And if our outside actions do not correctly tell what's inside, people will be disappointed because they expect Christians to reflect Christ. So let's do that this week wherever we are and whatever we say and do.

100

You Can't Change History

OBJECT: A board, nails, and a hammer.

LESSON: Everything we do becomes part of our history.

PRESENTATION: See this piece of board I have today? Now I'm going to take one of these nails and hammer it into the board. I'll do the same with another, and another, and another.

Now I'm going to pull out two of the nails. But the board isn't the same, is it? It has holes in it where those nails were.

Do you know what this illustrates? It reminds us that everything we do to ourselves becomes a part of our personal history. The nails I left in can represent the useful and good things I do, for sometimes I want nails to be in the board in order to hold it to something else. But sometimes the nails are useless and bad, and when I try to pull them out, the results of their uselessness show. The holes are still there. Everything I do to this board becomes part of its history.

History cannot be changed. However, we can learn from our mistakes. Sometimes you can fill holes with plastic wood and work hard to smooth the filler and color it to match the board. But if you go to all that trouble, you won't hammer a nail in that filled hole again. You have learned the lesson of how difficult it often is to correct the mistakes you make. So you can learn from mistakes—and you can sometimes correct them—but how much better it would be not to make the mistakes in the first place.

So ask God to forgive you, learn from your mistakes, and put into your life those things that will make it useful.